A BOOK ON THE OPEN THEATRE

A BOOK ON THE OPEN THEATRE

by ROBERT PASOLLI

THE BOBBS-MERRILL COMPANY, INC.
A Subsidiary of Howard W. Sams & Co., Inc.
Publishers/Indianapolis Kansas City New York

ACKNOWLEDGMENTS

I am grateful for financial assistance to the Ford Foundation and the Institute of International Education.

A portion of Chapter 6 appeared as part of my article "The Genesis of 'The Serpent'" in the *Village Voice*, February 20, 1969, to which thanks for permission to reprint.

The Bobbs-Merrill Company, Inc.
A Subsidiary of Howard W. Sams & Co., Inc.
Publishers / Indianapolis   Kansas City   New York

Copyright © 1970 by Robert Pasolli
All rights reserved
First printing
Library of Congress catalog card number 78-81296
Printed in the United States of America

Designed by Inese Burunovsky

To Michael Smith

CONTENTS

Prologue xiii

1   STARTING UP

Weapons 3
Colors 3
Sound-and-Movement in Lines 5
Sound-and-Movement with Partners 7
Sound-and-Movement in Couples 7

2   THE WORKSHOP AND THE ENSEMBLE

Inside-Outside 14
Walking in Space 16
Touching the Air 17
Passing and Receiving 17
Molding the Object 17
Imaginary Objects 17
Machines 18
Focus 18
Mirror Images 19
Transformation 20
Breathing and Talking Together 24
Organism 24
Trust in a Circle 25
Fingertip Trust 26
Blind Running 26
The Orchestra 27
Conductor in Circles 27

Conductor in Mass 28
Conductor in Lines 28
Conductorless Conductor 28
Conductor in Scenes 28
The Chord 32

3 THE WORKSHOP AND PERFORMANCE

Perfect People 37
Unnoticed Actions 38
The Taboo 39
Opposites 41
Influences 42
Life Styles 43
The Trial 44
"The Contest" 45
"The Illusion Scene" 46
Worlds 47

4 EXPANSION AND STRUGGLE

Sphere of Air 58
Radiating Energy 59
Molding the Air 59
Body Molding 59
Sense Adjustment 60
Stop-and-Start 72
Expecting 84

5 SUCCESS AND FAILURE

The Phrase 90
The Cat 97

The Big Tower   98
The Candle   99
The Small Tower   99
The Head Stand   99
The Shoulder Stand   100
Slow-Motion Walk   100
Tense-Up   100
Life Masks   102
Face Conversation   102

6 "THE IMPOSSIBLE STUDY"

Traveling, Turning, Falling   111
Shaking Out   111
Slow-Motion Wrestling   112
Breathing Bodies   113
Pulsing Bodies   113

Epilogue   127

"I would like to change my life and everyone else's. I don't know how to do it. If not the life, then the day, the evening, the hour, the minute." Joseph Chaikin

PROLOGUE

Joseph Chaikin: "My relationship to the theatre really changed while I was in Brecht's *Man Is Man* at the Living Theatre. I had gotten involved with the Becks as an actor to whom they offered a part—not a very good part: I was a replacement in *Many Loves*—but I thought it would lead to better parts with that on-going theatre, which was the only one in New York at the time. Then I would be seen and would be able to get out of there and do what I really wanted, which was Broadway. Judith and Julian cast me in *The Cave at Machpelah, Tonight We Improvise, In the Jungle of Cities,* and then, sometime later, had me take over the lead in *The Connection*. I wasn't very good in that part, although I did get better, but the Becks liked my performance, and they had me play it on the European tour in 1962. And I felt very swelled, like a minor star. . . . While we were in Europe, the Becks asked me to do Galy Gay in *Man Is Man*. They had the script along and I read it. There was going to be my real opportunity. Unless you're Lawrence Olivier and play anything you want, you only play a part like that once every ten years. I knew that the range of it required so much ability that if I could do it I'd be terrific. At the time I had an agent, but somebody told me that I should get a manager too. And I met this woman, and she said that she would manage me, and she started coming to rehearsals in order to make everything okay for me as the performer there. The Becks hated her, of course, and hated this thing that I was doing. But they would absorb anything. They were really amazing that way; they would absorb all kinds of things that would go on with people. Judith was directing the play, but then she decided

/ xiii

that the part of Widow Begbick was too good not to play it, and Julian took over the directing, so then *he* had to deal with my manager, always arbitrating for me and running up to the dressing room when I was the least bit unhappy. I fired her finally. I can't remember why; it was over nothing—something to do with changing the color of my hair for the role. She didn't want me to dye it, something like that; it had to do with something very dumb. She really had it in mind that I was going to go up a fancy tree. And I was prepared to have a very ascending career, and the Becks were prepared to have me use them in that way because I was the most likely person within the company to play Galy Gay.

"And it sounds like a fairy story, but it was in the playing of Galy Gay that I began to change. There I was, night after night, giving all my attention to pleasing, seducing, and getting applause from the audience, which is the very process wherein Galy Gay allows himself to be transformed from an innocent and good man into a thing, a machine—all because of flattery, one flattery after another. That's what really did it. Really. I'd go every night in front of the audience, and I'd give Brecht's speeches. I would stand next to the coffin which my old self was supposed to be buried in, and I'd talk about life and death—that all Galy Gay wanted was to go out and get a fish, but they offered him an elephant, and they shot him down. He was a good man, but I can't look in this box because I . . . I just can't; I'm afraid to see him. I'd do Brecht's lines again and again, and it made me *earnest* in a certain sense. And I started cutting out a lot of my fancy stuff, after having really brought the Becks into a confrontation with it and with a very temperamental me.

"All the while the Becks were doing the protest demonstrations, and I started to go along. I had been complaining since the day I walked into the Living Theatre: are you doing theatre or are you doing politics?—you know, that same argument which everyone gives them. And if you're doing this then do this, and if you're doing that then do that. And I'm sorry, and I'm a professional, and I'm such and such. But finally I was very involved with it. I started getting busted at peace things and sit-ins, and I felt a profound link with Brecht. And I felt enormously fulfilled in the performance night after night; no part has ever meant so much to me. You know, when people have given me any kind of praise about something I've done in directing or performing or anything, I've always felt fraudulent. I've always felt that it's like a stage set: it's not a real wall, it's a canvas. I would be glad that somebody liked it, but I felt that it wasn't what it seemed to be—it wasn't . . . substantial. But with *Man Is Man* people would tell me that it was good, or that it moved them, or that it meant something—and I felt that that was right. I got to the point where I was really talking to the audience, as Brecht would have it—something which I had learned absolutely never to do in any way. And I was a sort of new convert into a way of thinking. You know how converts are: they're so militant when they begin, as I was."

STARTING UP 1

The Open Theatre limped into existence during the first half of 1963. The first session of record occurred on February 1st in the borrowed auditorium of the Living Theatre. Seventeen actors and four writers declared themselves to be a new theatre group, did some warm-up exercises and two improvisations, and then went across the street for coffee. Throughout the spring they met more or less regularly, in discord and harmony. During the summer they went off in all directions, and whether the new group existed or not was at that point an open question.

The technique on which the Open Theatre subsequently built its aesthetic, however, was innovated during that first term. Joseph Chaikin devised the "sound-and-movement" procedure as a departure from the work of Nola Chilton, an acting teacher with whom most of the members had studied. Miss Chilton had closed her studio and expatriated to Israel late in 1962, and her core students started the Open Theatre as a framework within which to continue working together. Catherine Mandas was the dominant personality of this group, and it was she who approached Chaikin with the suggestion of starting the Open Theatre. Chaikin had been a member of the Living Theatre company since 1959. He had appeared in plays of Pirandello, Brecht, Jack Gelber, Paul Goodman, and William Carlos Williams. From experience he knew the demands which non-naturalistic plays make on actors and directors; he also knew the inability of the Living Theatre actors to meet those demands in a serious, craftsmanlike way. Twice he had started actors' workshops within the Living Theatre, but the constant state of emergency kept people away. With the new group of ex-Chilton students Chaikin found the opportunity to innovate techniques of acting and staging for non-naturalistic material.

Precisely how to develop the new techniques was not clear,

except that Chaikin knew to start from where the Open Theatre actors were; that is, from the Method and from Nola Chilton's variations on the Method. Miss Chilton, although one of the best teachers in New York, was a Method teacher like everybody else. She had evolved certain exercises to help actors deal with non-naturalistic material, however—a response to the assault by the Theatre of the Absurd, particularly, on the technique of the American actor. Miss Chilton had used a principle of physical adjustment, for example, as an actor's way-into-character for the plays of the Absurd, where character is not organized according to the principles of psychology familiar to Method actors. An instance was her exercise called "weapons" (more precisely, "weapon people"), where weapon imagery provided the actor with a démarche into non-psychological characterization.

WEAPONS
The actor lets the mode of operation of a particular weapon inform his physical behavior. A bazooka inspires lurching and bursting behavior; a rapier suggests thrusting movements. The actor does not try to convey the appearance of the weapon in use, but finds analogues in human behavior for the way the weapon operates.

$$\infty$$

Another of Miss Chilton's exercises was more difficult but more generally useful; it helped actors make physical adjustment to pure abstraction.

COLORS
One actor calls the colors and points to other actors, who must immediately make a movement and/or sound which is evoked by the color. The actors should respond impulsively

Note: A ∞ follows the description of each exercise.

without thinking. They succeed to the extent that they manage to make *some* physical adjustment to the abstraction. The exercise can be expanded to colors in phrases: barn-door red, instead of just red.

∞

The physical adjustment principle seems to have led to Chaikin's "sound-and-movement" technique, which became the Open Theatre's basic unit of expression. Chaikin had the actors do what amounted to physical adjustments to each other. From one actor in a pair he asked for a simple, sharply focused action with the voice and body, an impulsive action neither representative of everyday behavior nor expressive of inner feeling; a pure action, as it were. From the second actor, he asked for an impulsive re-creation of the first actor's statement, an appropriation of its dynamics and form; that is, a response in kind. The whole was to be a transmission of energy and a passing of kinetic material, but with the emphasis on the coming together of two actors who create a dramatic event by "inhabiting" the same kinetic environment. (I mean "kinetic," here and elsewhere, to refer to the body *and* the voice.)

The strategy of this innovation was significant. It corresponded to the strategy which the other arts had followed, decades before, in making the first moves away from the extant classical forms. Abstract painters and modern dancers expanded the field of expression in painting and dance by first assuming that the combination of any elements was artistically admissible. Thus they broke the links between artistic form and fixed doctrines of naturalistic representation and emotional expressiveness. Later and only secondarily did these innovators select certain elements within the expanded range which interested them as creators and did their work for them. In the development of the Open Theatre's post-naturalistic theatre technique, sound-and-movement was the first step: the actor used whatever actions he could produce on impulse with his physical instrument. Later in the group's career, specific kinds of sound-and-movement became the favored means of expression—the choice depending on the nature of the topic, insight, or vision under investigation in the workshop.

Since sound-and-movement is the core of the Open Theatre's particular vocabulary, the troupe continues to exercise the technique unaffected by the specific demands of particular workshop projects. Here is the basic structure for exercising sound-and-movement:

SOUND-AND-MOVEMENT IN LINES
The actors spread out in two facing lines about ten feet apart. Anyone begins the exercise by doing a sound-and-movement of any sort, and he repeats it over and over as he moves toward someone in the opposite line. That actor begins to do the same sound-and-movement as soon as he realizes that he has been chosen, moving out of his line to meet the approaching actor. The two share the action for a moment. Then the first actor moves into the second actor's place in line and drops the action. The second actor is now the principal. He transforms the sound-and-movement which he has received into something of his own, altering it radically or minimally according to his impulse. He moves across the open space, directing his sound-and-movement toward someone in the opposite line. They share it briefly, and then the third actor moves off on his own to repeat the process.

Certain things must be kept in mind. First, the "receiving" actor responds impulsively to the "giving" actor, sharing his action as if it were the only language which the two of them knew. Secondly, he evolves his own sound-and-movement out of the one he receives, acceding to impulse and avoiding conscious choice. (In a variant of these two points, the receiving actor reacts to the principal's sound-and-movement instead of appropriating and transforming it.) Thirdly, he should not try to look good; the values of the exercise are not those of performance.

∞

In regard to the "purity" of the action, elements of everyday movement and gesture and snatches of discursive speech are admissible; they are unavoidable. But while the actor need not block them he should avoid choosing them; he is supposed to work from impulse.

As for the relationship of sound-and-movement to emotional life, in principle, sound-and-movement is an abstract statement generated by kinetic impulse rather than emotional impulse. But while it does not come out of emotional experience, it does lead into it. The action, in short, engages the emotion rather than the other way around. Thus the actor must open himself to the emotional experience to which his action leads him; otherwise, as in all schools of acting, his work will be lifeless even if technically correct. One of the uses of the sound-and-movement exercise is to open the actor to the experience of emotions which are difficult for him; the kinetic statement which he receives from another actor may lie in alien emotional territory. Chaikin occasionally requires the company to deal with feelings which they have been instinctively avoiding by indicating a particular dynamic or emotional tone to which he asks the actors to adhere during the exercise.

The two other structures for exercising sound-and-movement are adaptations of the technique to predetermined emotion.

SOUND-AND-MOVEMENT WITH PARTNERS

The actors take random positions around the work space. Each actor chooses a "line" based on a clear feeling ("Mother loves me"; "tomorrow I get paid"). Then he seeks the expression of the line in sound-and-movement. The key word is "seeks." Rather than choosing and then executing an appropriate action, he *looks for* one while moving and sounding. When he has found one he moves toward any other actor and shows his statement. The partner responds by showing his own. The two then try to find a meeting point in their "dialogue," altering their individual statements to create one which they can share. If they cannot do it, they separate and take their statements to other actors.

∞

SOUND-AND-MOVEMENT IN COUPLES

Here the actors pair off before starting to work, decide on a line, and then work together to express the line in a shared action.

∞

Besides linking sound-and-movement to specified emotional values, these exercises confront the actor with the principle of seeking the physical expression of an emotion or attitude, rather than selecting it. This is the application in acting technique of the general principle that art is the image, not the result, of a process of investigation carried out by its creator. This basic concept of Chaikin's workshop research is discernible throughout the history of the troupe's work.

Although the sound-and-movement exercises are training exercises, the Open Theatre has occasionally done the sound-and-movement in lines exercise as an improvisational statement-of-principles before the public. Audiences seem to like it for its novelty, virtuosity, and energy. Its series of meetings and separations can also be taken as a metaphor for the human experience.

I have described sound-and-movement in its most developed form. During the Open Theatre's first term, of course, sound-and-movement was merely an embryonic technique. But it had significance in the internal politics of the troupe: it was the emblem of Chaikin's emerging leadership. The group had decided early that any member could set up and run his own project within the Open Theatre. Chaikin, however, was the only one to do it. Sessions which he did not dominate tended to be leaderless, and one can imagine the vacuum which his innovative abilities rushed to fill. In consequence, his theatrical interests, his professional values, his personal attitudes, his way of functioning in community began to set standards. Exactly what these standards were and are is the subject of the rest of this book, but for now the principle of technical innovation and the move beyond naturalism inherent in sound-and-movement will serve as indicators.

Some members of the group saw Chaikin's gathering hegemony as a usurpation. Miss Mandas spearheaded the drafting of a constitution in order to secure the concept of the Open Theatre as an extension of Nola Chilton's studio—in effect, an attempt to block Chaikin's dominance. The lengthy draft articles of the document became the focus of open disagreement among members. In the late spring, a full-scale crisis occurred, but at its height Miss Mandas left the group, a few others followed her out, and the constitution was shelved. That ended once and for all any attempts to structure the Open Theatre formally. It began, however, the long series of occasions on which differences within the group were resolved in Chaikin's favor.

THE WORKSHOP AND THE ENSEMBLE 2

The following fall Chaikin started a regular workshop, and the Open Theatre pulled together around it. Since then this workshop has been the core of the Open Theatre; the projects which other members have run from time to time have been incidental, tributary or short-lived. (The single exception was Megan Terry's *Viet Rock* workshop of 1965–66.) Indeed, the projects run by other members have characteristically depended for their vitality and staying power on Chaikin's attitude toward them.

Chaikin is the charismatic figure of the Open Theatre. His personal magnetism draws people into his orbit. The atmosphere is heady, the relationships intense. There is a feeling of anarchic freedom: Chaikin has a knack for stepping off-center, especially at times of controversy, and people feel their influence within the group to be equal. This is an illusion. Everything actually happens by Chaikin's instigation or sufferance. He maintains what you could call a diplomatic relationship with the group's affairs, both personal and practical; he has at his disposal considerable powers of personal address. He does not try to block differences and often accedes to them: over the years he has welcomed several people whose approaches to theatre, workshop, or group have opposed his own. He dislikes overt politics and avoids intervening directly in the relationships between the actors and a workshop leader, director, adviser, or writer. But when he feels strongly about something, his view finds an almost automatic adherence in the troupe. He lobbies subtly but effectively: his mood changes, he worries out loud, and the will of the troupe begins to change. He says that he hates to say "no" to anything, but rarely does he have to say it. As in most cohesive groups, the will of the members evolves in step with the will of the leader. At the Open Theatre, however, the members tend to be unaware of the fact that their will is a reflection of Chaikin's. Chaikin is the leader of the troupe but seems not to be; he controls practically everything while giving the impression of controlling practically nothing. It is important to see this clearly; it has shaped the work of the troupe.

I have said that Chaikin found in the Open Theatre the chance to innovate an acting and staging technique appropriate to non-naturalistic material. The plays of the absurdists, the poet-dramatists, Brecht, had increasingly preoccupied the American theatre in the 1950's and early 1960's, and Chaikin's workshop did concern itself with these texts. But the main thrust of the work, inspired and challenged by existing texts, went off in its own direction—and it is this work which has attracted a serious public regard to the Open Theatre beyond that which the troupe could have earned in producing extant scripts of the avant garde.

Chaikin is a philosophizer and a moralist, driven by the need to probe the confusions and anxieties of his living experience outside the theatre. He has made his workshop the beneficiary of this obsession.

> From Chaikin's notebooks:
>
> We have been taught in acting schools how singular are the emotions of a character—the simple, unilateral expression of sadness or happiness. Yet life is not like that. That's not what things seem to be, nor what I seem to be. Experience is richer, more complex, less ordered, more mysterious.... We have to try to express the complexity of things as we see them now, and to incorporate the confusion which we feel now. We have to explore the pleasure in despair and the fun in horror. When in the same city some men say that they are celebrating life and helping others, and other people say of the same way of life that

it is criminal, an actor has to understand the perplexing dichotomy. By understand, I mean to see—not simply to analyze, criticize and to sweep under the rug. We can do that by seeking the ways to make these things visible in action.

To make things visible in action has been the basic strategy of Chaikin's work over the years. The workshop approaches his questions, themes, and obsessions not through talking but through doing. Discussion is minimal. The emphasis is on improvising, and by structuring an improvisation Chaikin shapes the inquiry into the subject at hand. An Open Theatre piece emerges from an inquiry pursued in theatrical terms; it does not merely use theatrical terms to illustrate an inquiry conducted verbally and intellectually. One of the earliest inquiries of Chaikin's workshop will clarify this strategy.

"The Odets Kitchen" was an investigation into the reality behind surface behavior. Jean-Claude van Itallie, at the time a new writer and a member of Chaikin's workshop, wrote a short scene in the manner of the naturalistic playwrights. (It was named for Odets, but Chayevsky, Miller, or Inge would have done as well.) A mother, father, and daughter are stuck in their tiny New York apartment on a rainy day. Mother irons, father watches TV, and daughter mopes. To begin with, three actors simply performed the script, which was labeled the "outside."

Then, using the vocabulary of sound-and-movement, the same three actors improvised what they imagined to have been going on *behind* the external behavior of the three characters, but which the naturalistic mode of presentation had not made visible. They abstracted from the outside, distilled and explored the inner life of the given situation, looking for

12 / THE OPEN THEATRE

the characters' private miseries or fantasies and for the tensions or harmonies of the characters' relationships. The material could be closely related to what had occurred on the outside or it could be entirely divorced from it, depending on what the actors felt—not thought—to be relevant. This was called the "inside." After it, the actors performed the outside again.

Physicalization, through sound-and-movement, of a character's inner life is analogical; it represents inner experience where naturalism can only indicate it. In *The Three Sisters*, for example, Irina feels as though she is being stifled at the very moment that she should be starting to live. Everything is going wrong, and from her social behavior we get a sense of her anguish. But Chekhov cannot literalize Irina's inner state. The naturalistic genre does not allow it. Sound-and-movement, which is not tied to external behavior, can represent the forms, rhythms, and dynamics of the inner life with something like the power which they possess as experience. In the Odets scene, where the inside was framed by the outside, the *disparity* between the effectiveness of the two modes of presentation was discernible.

The inside, furthermore, being improvisational, was the means of *discovering* what existed in the inner realm. Because improvisation makes use of the actor's intuition, it taps the actor's own inner dimension, making available that which it is difficult to reach by rational process. For example, if in the outside Mother Odets expresses satisfaction at getting the ironing done, a correlative expression of relief does not necessarily follow in the inside improvisation. An actress might improvise on pain—developed from the heat of the iron—or intense frustration—developed from the monotonous motions of ironing. Or she might explore impulses unrelated to her chore, having to do with her husband or daughter. Different actors will discover different insides for the same character in the same setting of time and place.

"The Odets Kitchen," then, was one Open Theatre inquiry into the inner realm of human experience. Characteristically, it sought "to make visible in action" the subject under study. Also, it innovated a particular technique, called the "inside-outside," which the workshop could take up again as a useful tool when needed. Here are some general considerations of the "inside-outside."

INSIDE-OUTSIDE
The inside can be seen as the inner climate which the characters inhabit during the outside but which the actors can physicalize only through sound-and-movement separated from the naturalistic outside. The nature of this climate is what the inside improvisation explores. It may be parallel or contradictory to the outside. An inside statement can be individual or communal. Much of Chaikin's work has concentrated on the inner dynamic among the characters; that is, the inner impulses which feed the *relationships* of the characters of the outside. (See "The Odets Kitchen," pp. 12–14.)

Up to a point, it is helpful for the actor to think of the inside as the sub-text of the outside acted out. This will lead him to the inner realm of his character. But once there, he must distinguish things: the sub-text is verbal while the inside is non-verbal; the sub-text is concerned with psychological motivation, while the inside deals with emotional relations within the outside; the sub-text is usually contradictory to the text, while the inside may be parallel to the outside. When the inside is contradictory to the outside, its function is to reveal that which the outside left unexpressed. When the inside is parallel to the outside, usually its function is to state the values of the outside in larger terms.

When exercising the inside-outside, the actors who do the outside also do the inside. But as an exploration of inner realities, it is useful to have actors do the inside who have watched others do the outside. Another scheme is to have the inside and the outside improvised simultaneously by two sets of actors. In this last case, each actor in the second set can relate his inside statement to a specific actor in the first set; or the matter can be left undefined, so that three actors must capture the inside of an outside being done by four or five other actors. The inside-outside is useful in building ensemble techniques.

As a performance device, inside-outside turned up in van Itallie's *Interview*. In the Politician scene toward the end of the play, bystanders break out of the crowd individually and in couples to meet the candidate. They "speak" to him in sounds and movements which are really insides to scenes the actors had done earlier in the play—reprises of the characters' former experience, as it were. The candidate, however, responds to them naturalistically, with remarks like "Indeed yes, the air we breathe is foul. . . . I agree with you wholeheartedly. . . ." The disparity of language underscores the separation between the people and the polity.

In addition to the exercises and the improvisational structures which Chaikin has evolved in his workshop, the Open Theatre has borrowed freely from extant techniques, particularly the newer ones of Viola Spolin, Jerzy Grotowski, Joseph Schlichter. In the early days, it was a principle of the workshop that members should teach each other what they had learned elsewhere. Among the first things the group took up were the theatre games of Viola Spolin, which Chaikin had encountered during the summer of 1963 while working with the Second City play production unit in Chicago.

Although the workshop concentrated on games for only a few weeks, the work was very helpful in breaking down the hold of the Method over the actors. Games kineticize the actor, providing easy and enjoyable structures to start him moving and using his body. Games recapture the inventiveness and suppleness of the child. Some of them emphasize sensory experience, but many of them are task exercises; thus they feed the tendency away from psychology and toward action. A handful of them remain in the Open Theatre canon, which new members of the troupe work through. As they were appropriated from Miss Spolin, however, several of them lost their precise correspondence to her techniques. What follows are really Open Theatre exercises with a debt for inspiration to Viola Spolin. (For these and other exercises according to Miss Spolin, see her book *Improvisation for the Theatre*.)

WALKING IN SPACE

This exercise aims at making the actor aware of space and of his presence in it. The company walk around the working area and concentrate on how their bodies occupy, fill, displace, and vacate the space. They shift their attention from one part of the body to another: the head, trunk, knees, and so forth, not just the arms and legs. To reinforce their sensitivity, they later move around without thinking about the space. The simplicity with which this exercise can be described belies its usefulness in developing the actor's kinetic sensitivity.

The actors can also be asked to imagine that the quality of the space changes—from air to grease, bubble gum, foam rubber. They must adjust their movements to these changes.

∞

TOUCHING THE AIR

Here the actor applies his increased awareness of space as a substance. He touches the air, leaving an imprint on it, using various parts of his body. Then he shapes the air, using all parts of his body to alter the contour of the mass of air. Two actors can work together, shoving the air around, enclosing themselves in it, and so forth.

∞

PASSING AND RECEIVING

The actors throw around an imaginary ball. They consider it to be transforming regularly from a beachball to a medicine ball and back again. Thus the ball is heavy when tossed and light when caught. The receiver makes the adjustment.

∞

MOLDING THE OBJECT

The actors stand in a circle and pass around an imaginary globe. Each actor alters its shape before passing it on. Peter Feldman defines the aim here as "experiencing the plasticity of the object and visualizing the changes."

∞

IMAGINARY OBJECTS

Here the actors deal with specific imaginary objects—tools, toys, and the like. The important thing is that the actor experience the object through using it, rather than through his sensory experience of it as in molding the object. The actors are in a circle. One begins the exercise by discovering an object through using it, then passes it to the next actor, who experiences the object by using it, and then transforms it into a different object and passes that to the next person.

This exercise gets actors used to the principle of things changing in mid-course (see the "transformation" exercise).

∞

MACHINES

One actor starts this exercise by doing a sound and/or movement representing a moving part of a machine. When another actor recognizes which machine, he adds a sound and/or movement representing another part of it. Other actors join in when they recognize anything already established. The exercise does not aim at re-creating an actual machine, as does Miss Spolin's "parts of the whole," from which it derives, but at creating a new, inexistent one. Thus, it is not necessary for an actor *correctly* to recognize what is under way, but merely to have in mind a definite mechanical function related to what the others are doing. The actors should make simple and precise sounds and movements.

The Open Theatre has done a great deal with machines as metaphorical statements. The opening and closing improvisations in Megan Terry's play *Keep Tightly Closed in a Cool Dry Place* illustrate the relationships of the three characters and tell something about the condition which they share. Chaikin has used machines to explore social roles: imagining society to be a machine, the actors searched for the mechanical part in it which a doctor would play, a street-cleaner, an intellectual, a congressman. The machine device also enables actors to contribute to a setting. An example is the Telephone Operator scene in *Interview*, where the actors mime the action of the electronic circuitry.

∞

FOCUS

Two, three, or four improvised scenes are set in motion at the same time. As the actors improvise they pass the focus of attention back and forth from scene to scene: the actors in one scene make the dynamics of whatever they are doing more defined; at the same time, the actors in the other scene blunt what they are doing. Thus as one group fades, another group comes into focus. The trick is for the actors to give and take the focus instinctively. The actors who are not in focus nonetheless keep their scenes going both verbally and physically, but at reduced intensity. Each scene continues without interruption from the start of the exercise until the end, although it must rise and fall in intensity according to the shifting focus.

This exercise develops the actors' capacity to attend to what is going on around them while carrying forward their own actions. It is necessary to keep the scene ideas simple: job interviews, couples conversing at parties, groups at restaurant tables.

∞

MIRROR IMAGES

The actors work in pairs, defining the plane of a mirror between themselves by touching their fingertips together. One actor is "real," the other the image. After a time they break the fingertip contact in order to do more elaborate actions. Later they switch roles.

A variant is done by leaving it indeterminate which partner is the person, which the reflection. They lead and follow each other, taking care to stay coordinated, which is the point of the exercise.

In "fun-house mirrors," two actors face each other a short distance apart. One performs simple, everyday actions, and the other re-creates them as if he were the image in a distorting mirror. This exercise develops the actor's ability to evolve grotesque actions out of normal behavior; that is, to base invention on observed phenomena.

∞

TRANSFORMATION

A transformation is a radical change in the circumstances of an improvisation made by the actors improvising. For example: two actors are teenage brothers arguing over who gets to sleep in the lower bunk of their new double-decker bed. Claims, counterclaims; threats, entreaties. Abruptly the older brother starts acting like a wild animal, say, a lion. He has transformed his identity. His partner must transform too. He might become a small animal trapped by the lion or, conversely, a hunter stalking the lion. His change in identity establishes a new set of circumstances, which he and his partner then elaborate improvisationally.

Several things are important. The actors must let things happen; that is, they must follow their instincts, breaking out of the established circumstances as frequently and freely as they can. They must accept whatever changes their partners initiate, finding a way to join in; they must cooperate with even bewildering changes.

Transformation taps the unconscious resources of the actor, who, in jumping from one set of circumstances to another, relies on links between given and potential situations which he would not necessarily understand rationally. Thus the device mines levels of meaning in a given situation which might not be otherwise evident. Transformation is a way rapidly and with minimal discussion to invent situations for improvisation (where improvisation itself is the goal). In terms of acting training, transformation develops the actor's ability to handle a wide range of situations, acting styles, and emotions. It also heightens the actor's sensitivity to partners.

Since transformation takes the actor out of himself, it is a very good way to break the grip of the Method and the dependence on psychological motivation and logical transition between situations which it imposes on the actor. Transformation frees the actor to be the child (now I'm the grass, now I'm the queen, now I'm the king of the mountain, now I'm a cloud).

In transformation, the actor is not limited to changing his identity (the who). He can change the place of action (the where), the clock time or epoch (the when), or the relationship between himself and his partners as defined by what goes on between them (the what). In fact, transforming the who often automatically entails other changes. In exercising transformation, it is useful to limit the change to one element, for this makes greater demands on the actors. In such cases, however, it is important for the actor initiating a transformation to leave it somewhat undefined, so that his partner has some latitude in getting himself into the new circumstances. As an improvisation, however, transformation is richest when the choices for change are wide open. Here the actor's unconscious cues can function most fully. As such, the improvisation can include machines, animals, and personified abstractions as well as recognizable characters. The Open Theatre has frequently presented "open transformations" in public as ensemble improvisations.

During a "style transformation" the theatrical or sociological style of a scene is transformed (restoration comedy to soap opera to Brechtian *lehrstücke* to Hollywood melodrama) in the course of an improvisation. The "singing transformation" is a variation of the style transformation in which the actors improvise on a line of text or brief dialogue, perhaps from a scene in progress (madrigal to Verdi aria to hillbilly croon).

"Rescue-squads" is a device where an actor or actors enter an improvisation as it is flagging, transforming the situation as they go in. The original actors stay or leave depending on their instincts for fitting into the situation initiated by the rescue-squad. These ensemble improvisations are entertaining virtuoso pieces. But the fullest development of the transformation device occurs in connection with playwriting and character conception, for which see Megan Terry's plays *Calm Down Mother* and *Keep Tightly Closed in a Cool Dry Place*.

∞

In the work so far discussed, particularly in the transformation, the sound-and-movement, and the inside-outside, the ensemble dynamic, which has become the mark of Open Theatre style, is already obvious.

Ensemble acting in the traditional theatre is a concern for the orchestral relationship of the characters. It came of a reaction to the 19th century operatic tradition wherein productions were built around one or two star players for whom the lesser characters served as a kind of chorus to their star turns. Chekhov's naturalism, as implemented by Stanislavski and beyond, depended on a greater equality of the roles and a greater emphasis on exchange between characters. The lead actors were played down, and the minor characters up; the concern was with a total harmonious effect rather than with individual virtuosity.

But ensemble in this tradition still depends on character, and hence on the actor's absorption in self. Even Shakespeare can be produced within this tradition. Ensemble at the Open Theatre, however, is another matter entirely.

Where things are organized not according to the demands of character, but to those of incident and situation, it is possible for the actor to avoid working on himself. Instead he works off what is occurring around him; his source is without rather than within himself. He works *from* himself; that is, from his impulses, but those are a response to the event within which he exists. Since from his point of view the event is what the other actors are doing, his impulses occur as responses to his fellow actors. Whether a response is reproductive or reactive, the actor exists in ensemble relationship to his fellow actors.

In sound-and-movement, the actors meet by sharing the dynamics or form of an action. In the inside portion of the inside-outside, they search for the communal dynamic which exists without expression in the outside. In transformations, they find ways to come together over and over in the rapidly altering circumstances. The enabling factors are the kinetic impulse toward action and the avoidance of character aesthetics.

The motor which drives Chaikin's pursuit of ensemble aesthetics is best identified by his own words:

> Ensemble asserts the way that people are alike. We live and die separate. But there is a point where we are completely interlocked, a point where we are brought together, all of us, by our participation in nature, where we are brought together two by two, or in threes or fours, by our participation in something larger than each of us.

Several Open Theatre exercises build the actors' abilities in ensemble playing.

BREATHING AND TALKING TOGETHER

Several actors stand in a line side by side, relax and concentrate on breathing in unison. Someone who is not participating asks a question to which each actor in the line responds with his own answer, but taking care to start and stop talking in unison with the others. The questions should be simple but allow for ample answers ("what did you do yesterday?"; "what does your wife look like?"). The exercise continues until all the actors in the line are starting and stopping in unison. To do this, the actors must split their attention between what they are saying themselves and the vocal impulses of those next to them. It is not important to finish an answer, only to stop talking when the others do.

As an exercise, breathing and talking together has no leader. As an improvisation, the person in the middle of the line is the catalyst for the others, the impulses passing from actor to actor from the middle of the line out toward both ends.

∞

ORGANISM

Organism is related to breathing and talking together. Five or so actors link arms in a line. Moving around the space, they try to become a unit; that is, each member of the line tries to accommodate himself to the movement impulses coming to him from the others. The actors avoid leading the others or feeding them impulses, but rather they follow each other.

In an elaboration of this exercise, two organisms are set up at the same time. After each has gotten itself together, they go to encounter each other. The actors should let whatever happens happen: hostility, assault, cooperation, merging. They should go with the impulses of their organism, neither leading nor resisting them. Sounds may be used at the same time.

∞

A sense of responsibility toward other actors and the emotional ability to rely on them are two matters germane to ensemble playing. They cannot be willed into being, but a little work in their direction yields disproportionate results. They are correlatives, and each will develop out of the other. Of the score of known trust exercises, the Open Theatre uses three in particular.

TRUST IN A CIRCLE
This is widely known as a party game. From five to eight actors make a circle around another actor, who stands relaxed but not limp and with his eyes shut. Keeping his feet firmly planted and the plumb line of his body straight, he leans forward, backward or sideways until he loses his balance and falls into the arms of the actors in the circle, who catch him and set him back up. The catchers must find just the right moment to take hold of the falling actor—too soon and he won't experience the fall; too late and he'll hit the floor. The idea is for him to fall but not to fall down. (This consideration governs how large the circle is made.) After one actor has fallen several times in different directions, he joins the catchers, and another actor takes his turn in the center.

The catchers have a collective responsibility, as well as an individual one. It is not sufficient for one person to catch the falling actor; those at his sides must help since someone falling is dead weight. The catchers must deserve the trust of the falling actor, who for his part must push through his fear, if he has any. As simple as the exercise sounds, it requires concentration and cooperation.

∞

FINGERTIP TRUST

Each actor chooses a partner and they touch their fingertips together (the ten of one against the ten of the other). One of them closes his eyes, and the other leads him around the room, turning, swooping, going now fast, now slow, kneeling down, climbing over things—making his actions as varied as possible without breaking the fingertip contact. The sighted actor must take care to keep his charge from tripping or bumping into things or colliding with other couples; at the same time he must try to get him to be more and more venturesome. The "blind" actor must give himself over to his partner's care and control. Each must concentrate on the other and respond to his rhythms and impulses. After a while, they switch roles.

∞

BLIND RUNNING

This is also done in pairs. The sighted actor grasps his blind partner firmly by one hand and runs him around the room as fast as possible. He must use the same concentration and attention as in fingertip trust. The blind actor must make an effort to rely on his partner. After a time, they switch roles.

∞

The single most important ensemble device of the Open Theatre is the "conductor." Three things can be done as a warm-up to it, although they are not necessary. One is to use recorded music, as Nola Chilton did, to influence the actor's emotional climate and hence his behavior during improvisation. Another preliminary is Viola Spolin's metronome exercise, where the actors match the pacing of an improvisation to various settings on the metronome. The third preliminary, which the Open Theatre consistently uses, is its own "orchestra" exercise.

THE ORCHESTRA

This exercise requires a group of actors to express in sound what one of them expresses in movement. The conductor does not imitate the baton-waving of the symphony conductor, but employs his entire body to feed rhythmic impulses to the others, who face him in a semicircle. They are the orchestra, but their instruments are their voices. Their job is to find vocal analogues to the conductor's movements. Though they do not need to avoid imitating the sounds of musical instruments, they should not limit themselves. The more inventive the conductor is the better. Yet he must not become so absorbed in his invention that he loses control over the orchestra; he must indicate which actors he wants to respond to a given action, for how long, and so on. The actors in the orchestra do not move; the conductor makes no sounds. The procedure of the exercise can be reversed, with the orchestra doing analogues in movement to the sounds made by the conductor.

∞

The principle of the conductor device is clear in the orchestra exercise: it is the appropriation of the kinetic impulses of another's action, but not, as in the sound-and-movement exercises, its form. Where sounds and movements are separated in the orchestra exercise, however, they are combined in all of the conductor exercises.

CONDUCTOR IN CIRCLES

This is the simplest structure of the conductor exercise. The actors group around the conductor. He does an action of any sort in sound-and-movement, and the others respond spontaneously with sounds and movements of their own, appropriating the rhythm and dynamics of the conductor's action, but avoiding imitating its form. Sensitivity, not virtuosity, is the aim. Each actor in the circle takes a turn as conductor.

∞

CONDUCTOR IN LINES
Here the actors stand side by side in a straight line with the conductor in the middle or at either end. They respond to his dynamics as fully as they can.

∞

CONDUCTOR IN MASS
To establish this structure, it is necessary merely to avoid setting up a circle or a line. The group sits together on the floor, or stands together in a bunch. The workshop leader names someone as the conductor, and as he moves the others adopt the pulse of his actions as the basis for their own. Everyone must focus on the conductor, wherever he moves to. When the workshop leader names another actor to take over as conductor, the group simply shifts its focus and works off the new person.

∞

CONDUCTORLESS CONDUCTOR
This is very difficult. No specific person is the conductor. The actors must be sensitive to the impulses of the group as a whole, and follow along as its rhythm, intensity and dynamics evolve. No one must lead, but everyone should appropriate the impulses which he senses around himself.

The conductorless conductor exercise makes great demands on the actors' sensitivity, and it cannot be done by people who haven't mastered the simpler conductor exercises. Evolving it out of the conductor in mass exercise—the workshop leader merely says "no conductor" in mid-exercise—is helpful, as that is a time when the actors are already working off each other.

∞

CONDUCTOR IN SCENES
This is the conductor device adapted to scene improvisation. Two, three, or four actors decide on a simple situation

as the subject for a naturalistic improvisation, and they set to work. Another actor, designated as the conductor and standing to the side, does sounds and movements. The actors in the scene use the dynamics of the conductor's action in their own actions. Not only must they adapt what they do to the conductor's impulses, they must also allow his impulses to *determine* what they do. For example, if a conductor is doing an easy, relaxed sound-and-movement for a scene between two couples at dinner, the actors will probably engage in quiet conversation. As the conductor intensifies his sound-and-movement, they will naturally grow more animated and volatile in their conversation. But following the impulse fully would mean breaking loose from the conversation: starting an argument, throwing food at each other, upsetting the table, and so on. The actors must not stint on using the conductor's impulses; the point of the exercise is to make fullest use of his material. For his part, the conductor should take cues from the developments of the scene and give the actors impulses which are usable; otherwise, the exercise will be little more than a good workout.

It is possible to use two conductors, one on either side of the work space; half of the actors follow one, the other half the other. This is advanced and requires some virtuosity. It is also possible for one of the actors *within* the scene to function as the conductor.

Since the actors in the scene must divide their attention between the developing line of their improvisation and the impulses coming from the conductor, they should choose banal situations on which to improvise and should not burden themselves with intricate dialogue. Banal does not mean trivial, however. Here are some random suggestions made by Megan Terry at one work session: a mother is throwing her daughter out of the house for refusing to drop her hippie friends; a man is sitting up all night with a friend to keep him from committing suicide; a man and his wife are getting ready to go to a party with her liberal friends where she expects her husband's conservatism will embarrass her.

∞

The conductor in scenes exercise, although in a sense the most complex of the conductor exercises, was the one which Chaikin developed first. His explanation of how it came about throws light on the technique:

> I was in a room with some people, and everybody was having a good time, except one person who was in terrible anguish. And I thought that if the rest of us could empathize with him for just a second—if we could enter not into the content of what bothered him, but into the pulse of it—then we would be able to console him, and that it would be good for us too. I thought up the conductor in scenes exercise when Joyce and Barbara were doing a scene about a boarding house. They couldn't sleep, and they came down from their rooms and met. I assigned a conductor to their scene to see what would happen. The results confirmed a direction we had been moving in, so we went back to sound-and-movement and worked out the conductor exercises in order.

These exercises of the conductor device are extremely important to the Open Theatre's practice of ensemble. Not only do they focus the actor on the actions of others, but they make the important distinction between sharing an impulse and imitating an action. Imitating is one of the big problems in all theatre work; everybody talks about it, from Stanislavski to Grotowski. The point is that life and vitality occur on the stage when the actor discovers his forms for himself, and does not duplicate someone else's. At the Open Theatre, actors new to the conductor exercises will imitate each other's actions. Even experienced members of the troupe do poorly after neglecting the conductor exercises; if they manage to avoid duplicating forms, they fall into a subtler kind of imitating—that of expressing attitudes, rather than exploring. The conductor exercises are valuable precisely because they break this down; they are the essential ensemble exercises at the Open Theatre.

One of the advantages of ensemble is the sense of security it gives the actor, who perceives that he is not alone. Especially in front of an audience, this can release a certain energy from the anxiety of isolation, a factor which reviewers of public performances of the Open Theatre have noted in their enthusiasm for the troupe's pyrotechnics. Ensemble has the advantage, in other words, of freeing the actor from some standard limitations.

At the Open Theatre, the aesthetics of ensemble interlocks with the politics of ensemble; that is, with the troupe's way of being together.

> From Chaikin's notebooks:
>
> I believe that one can do in his art what he can't do in his life. I believe that there are ways of being outside the profession in order to be inside one's experience as an artist. I believe that we are on our own in trying to expand and develop ourselves, but it is all in vain unless we collaborate together and pool for an ensemble.

From the Living Theatre, the Open Theatre inherited a distaste for the established, bourgeois norms, professional as well as social. But the Open Theatre's stance has been less that of defiance, which the Living Theatre has carried so far, than that of independence. Independence takes work to maintain because of the lures of coöptation, if not downright capitulation, particularly the professional lures of careerism and making-it, and Chaikin has a habit of worrying these matters out loud.

The Open Theatre is exclusionist. The ties between the members are not those of evangels but of monastics. Worried about contamination, Chaikin has been reluctant to take the troupe out into the world. Another inheritance, Nola Chilton's emphasis on the therapeutic value of workshop, has also helped keep the walls of the workshop repaired.

But if the Open Theatre is a kind of huddle, the relationships in the huddle are not personal relationships, but working relationships. The members of the troupe relate through the work rather than through direct personal encounter and, except in special cases, do not associate closely in their personal lives. The work of the troupe, however, *does* involve the exposure of personal material in personal revelation and exchange.

The cohesion of the group and the ensemble aesthetic are expressed and reinforced by "the chord," a ritual devised by Chaikin, which Jacques Levy observed to be the emblem of the Open Theatre, standing for its form and its content.

THE CHORD

I stand in a circle with the other actors, my arms around the shoulders of the people next to me, their arms around my waist. I close my eyes, relax and listen. I hear breathing— from the others, from myself. I listen to it and feel it. It is regular and hypnotic. It turns into a drone, and I drone too.

Now it is a humming, and I hum. It rises and gets louder and then falls back to a soft dissonance in which I can distinguish my own voice and, if I try, the voices of my two neighbors. I can hear it all around me; I am within it. I match myself to it. I don't want to alter it, but to let it alter me. I no longer know where I am physically. I no longer remember who is at my right and left, although we are holding each other. The communal sound is dying out. But then it starts up again, droning louder, and again I go with it. But it dies back fast. I hear breathing again. I wait, relaxed and listening. Chaikin says "okay" quietly; I open my eyes and see feet in a circle. Looking up and dropping my arms, I see Brenda and Paul next to me; I remember them now.

∞

The chord affirms the Open Theatre as a collective. In it, the actor perceives the group as an entity of which he is a part. He experiences "I" in "it," rather than "you" or "them." The actor is in the group, but alone in it; the chord does not submerge his ego but subsumes it.

The chord closes its circle to observers, keeping its meaning inside. Observers find it unfruitful to watch it happen; furthermore, their presence is inhibitive since it tempts the actors to perform. An actor performing in the chord will try to lead the group impulse, rather than accede to it; this will abort the chord, which has followers but no leaders.

THE WORKSHOP AND PERFORMANCE 3

Participation in Chaikin's workshop is not limited to actors. Playwrights, critics and other directors often take part. Chaikin looks for interplay with another mind to check out his plans for larger moves. Over the years, various friends have worked closely with him: directors Peter Feldman, Jacques Levy and Roberta Sklar; critics Gordon Rogoff and Richard Gilman; writers Megan Terry, Jean-Claude van Itallie, and Michael Smith.

The relationship of the writer to Chaikin's workshop is elusive. It has changed from project to project and from writer to writer, and it is obscured by the day to day interactions of twenty to thirty people. What is constant in the relationship, however, is the fact that the writer participates in the workshop before writing anything down. The writer is defined not by the fact that he has written a script on which the work is based, as in the case of traditional production, but on the fact that he *will* write a script related to the work which the troupe is improvising. When the work is done and ready to be shown publicly, one can look back and say that the writer structured the workshop investigation to make it understandable to outsiders. In doing so, he asserted his own personality and vision, to the extent sometimes of radically altering the actors' private investigation. However, three things keep the writer in touch with the vision originally articulated by Chaikin and the actors: one, already mentioned, is his presence during their research; another is Chaikin's presence, usually as stage director, during the rehearsals after the preparation of the script and before the public presentation; the third is the fact that the actors preparing to perform are the same actors who did the workshop research.

In the early days, the relationship between the workshop and the writers was very close. The directors asked the writers to write *for* the troupe, to tailor some writing to the specific matters of concern in the workshops. That Miss Terry and van Itallie have done this so well is what has enabled the Open Theatre to ignore extant scripts and so to become a creating theatre rather than merely a producing one.

Van Itallie's relationship with the troupe has been the closer and more consistent and has lasted longer. This has to do with his close and special friendship with Chaikin, but also with his abilities to help Chaikin *clarify* his investigations early in their undertaking. He has contributed to the workshop not only in making the researches accessible to the outside public, but also in structuring things toward which the workshop was only groping, clarifying things for Chaikin and the actors themselves. "The Odets Kitchen" is one example. The artistic success of Open Theatre work is a benefit of van Itallie's close collaboration and participation in the formative day to day work.

Here we should take up some improvisational investigations of that early period. Among the questions which Chaikin posed in the workshop were many having to do with social behavior. Much of Chaikin's work has an existential bias; it takes behavior rather than ideas as the source of insight into the world.

PERFECT PEOPLE
The perfect people was the first Open Theatre investigation to have any social significance, even though it was facile and comic. It has to do with the conditioned person.

Perfect people are the sanitized, regularized, and glamorized types which the image-makers have us all secretly believing we ought to be—those clean-cut men and virginal women who live a kind of half-life with double intensity in the magazine advertisements and television commercials. Imagining that these beings had continuous life, the actors improvised scenes from the "perfect lives" which they would lead. Particular kinds of perfect people were created, such as the perfect teenager, the perfect secretary, the perfect cowboy. Frequently, perfect people were placed in incongruous situations, like battlefields, prisons, and funeral parlors. In one format, some normal, messy people were put in prison to be perfected. Another format became a public presentation known as "The Party." Among a group of perfect people the only means of communication was in advertising slogans ("It's what's up front that counts," etc.). Each actor had a different one to use as he went about behaving as the perfect guest—impervious, bland, synthetic. One actress, however, was imperfect; that is, normal. Compared to the others she was extremely sensitive and vulnerable. She did not have a slogan, and so was unable to relate to the others despite her very great effort. The perfect guests built up a frenzy of dancing, laughing, and shouting out their slogans, and eventually made a victim of the normal guest by throwing her, quite perfectly, into the swimming pool, where she drowned.

The Open Theatre uses this improvisation as an exercise to awaken actors to degrees of aliveness, which helps them realize the reliance of conventional acting on easy formulas of characterization. There are many kinds of perfection to pursue: jet-set perfect, middle-class-midwestern perfect, every-actor's-ideal-of-himself perfect, etc.

∞

UNNOTICED ACTIONS

In this improvisation several actors establish a social event—a community meeting, cocktail party, etc.—and carry it forward *verbally* in the polite manner and with the degree of formality appropriate to such occasions. As soon as they have it under control, they begin to act out impulses which usually exist only in one's fantasy and which one normally suppresses: they pick noses, climb on shoulders, pull hair, look under dresses, remove clothing. But they continue the socially correct dialogue of the meeting or party and do not register surprise or dismay at each other's unusual behavior.

The improvisation brings two contradictory worlds into being, and the actor must inhabit and contribute to the development of both at once. In order to limit the demands on the actors, it is practical to choose a well-known situation as the social construct.

Unnoticed action improvisations are most entertaining when the social context is driest, which puts the sexual or hostile behavior in sharpest relief. In performance, the Open Theatre usually turns this improvisation into a free-for-all. But the improvisation also makes a serious point about our social behavior, by making the normally unexpressed contradictions to it visible. Van Itallie used the principle of the unnoticed action in *Interview* with a symbolic point. The interviewers examine the teeth, hair, and underarms of the applicants while asking them the usual questions in the usual tone about their former employment, which the applicants answer as if nothing were out of the ordinary.

∞

THE TABOO

The unnoticed action improvisation does not represent a real-life situation; bizarre behavior would attract attention and disrupt a real meeting or party. The taboo improvisation takes this fact as its premise. Any social situation depends for its existence on the order and balance of its elements; thus, any circumstance which disrupts them will undermine the situation. The purpose of the taboo improvisation is to find out what circumstances must not be introduced if a given social situation is to survive. When an actor has sensed what the taboo is for the improvised situation, he deliberately plays it out.

For example, some actors improvise a scene about businessmen commuting to the suburbs. They are tired, irritable, and uncommunicative. They read newspapers, play cards, and complain about their jobs. This then is the situation. Suddenly an actor puts his head in his neighbor's lap and goes to sleep. There is a certain logic here; weariness and a degree of fellowship are components of the situation. But the established relationships of the characters do not permit this behavior. The actor's choice has tipped the balance of the elements of the situation; he has found the taboo, or one of them.

Michael Smith submitted the following examples to the workshop, with the taboos already identified: the bank teller must not treat money as if he thought it were just so many scraps of paper; the lover must not refer to his income tax while making love; the host must not indicate that his guests are all dull, stupid, or of no use to him; the priest must not show that he doubts God while saying Mass.

As an exercise, the taboo is done as follows: two or more actors set up a situation which they wish to examine for its inherent disruptive circumstance. They search the taboo out while improvising, and when one of them feels he has found it, he performs it, thus breaking down the situation which had been established. The exercise can also be done without choosing specific situations beforehand. The company divides into twos or threes, and the first team runs into the work area, one member calling out a locale as he goes, say a supermarket or a doctor's waiting room. They begin improvising and looking for the taboo inherent in whatever situation develops. As quickly as they can, they act out the taboo and leave the work area. The next team runs in.

Sexual taboos, being on everybody's mind, are quick to emerge in this improvisation, but the subtler social, religious, and ethical taboos are worth researching. Taboo improvisations tend to be entertaining, as they are often funny, witty, and surprising; but, like the unnoticed action improvisation, the Open Theatre has at times used the structure as a serious investigation. You could call the taboo an unnoticed action noticed.

∞

OPPOSITES

This is an exercise which takes the contradiction mechanism of the unnoticed action improvisation a step further; its purpose is to locate the tension between the verbal and physical life of a character. The actor, working alone, tries to express one quality with his voice and an opposing quality with his body. It is like the children's game of patting the head while rubbing the stomach, except that one action is verbal, the other physical. The enabling mechanism of the exercise is the rhythmic element common to the contradictory statements. The best example I have seen occurred in workshop when Lee Worley sang "Whistle a Happy Tune" while writhing on the floor in agony. She got a jerky rhythm going and then used it as the motor for both physical agony and vocal lightheartedness.

There were some attempts to build opposites into scenes. Smith devised a scheme in which the actors were to contradict in their physical life the emotional values of a scene. An example would be when two actors keep emotional tension going between them while moving around jauntily. Aimed at making the psychic and physical life of the scene independent of each other, the scheme observed the Brechtian principle that elements of a scene are heightened when you break the usual relationships between them. Another attempt was devised by van Itallie. The actors were guests at a cocktail party. Wagnerian music blared from the phonograph, and the actors responded to it physically. But in what they said to each other they maintained the cool sophistication characteristic of cocktail parties.

∞

INFLUENCES

Influences is an extension of the principle of perfect people. It seeks to visualize the influence of our past experiences on what we do in the present. To what extent is a person's behavior influenced by the fairy tales which he learned as a child, by the writings of Sartre or Salinger which he encountered as a student, or by the *Reader's Digest*, which he has read every month for years? What about Bible stories, soap opera, the movies, 1930's liberalism?

Two or more actors improvise a naturalistic scene in such a way that the choices which they make as characters will illuminate a predetermined influence. To parody the influencing phenomenon is not the point, but rather to make its presence in the character's mentality visible through his actions and statements.

The perfect people improvisation can be considered an influence improvisation: it makes visible the influence on the characters of the behavior of people in advertisements.

∞

LIFE STYLES

This improvisation looks into the similarities and differences between the life styles of various groups of people. A spatial adjustment is utilized. Each of three or four separated areas marked out on the workshop floor is assigned to a specific life style, such as urban Black, midwestern middle-class, and Asian peasant. A team of actors is assigned to each area. Each team improvises an elementary story, such as a marriage proposal, according to the style designated in its area. Usually the story is broken down into its components: (1) the boy arrives at the girl's house, (2) he gets rid of her parents, (3) he offers her a ring, (4) she turns him down. The first component is played out in each area before the second component is taken up. This procedure makes the contrasts in behavior from area to area abundantly clear.

As is the case with many of the Open Theatre's improvisations, an easy leap to entertainment can be made. At the Cafe La MaMa in 1965, the troupe presented a life styles improvisation of which the subject was "the boy leaves home." Tarzan, Jane and Boy were in one area; Ozzie, Harriet, and Ricky Nelson in another; and Joseph, Mary, and Jesus in a third. Each of the boys left to seek his fortune, but then decided to return home. They got mixed up, however, and wandered into the wrong homes: Christ encountered Ozzie and Harriet; Joseph and Mary had to handle Boy; Tarzan and Jane met Ricky Nelson.

∞

But Chaikin was more interested in ways in which behavior was alike from style to style rather than different; he used the life styles improvisation as a means to focus on the common ground of widely differing groups of people. The life styles improvisation makes it clear that many events do not differ in their essentials from culture to culture. Social roles or functions are involved, rather than persons. In a wedding, there has to be a bride and a groom. To what degree, then, is a person's behavior determined by his social role, rather than by the dictates of his character? The transformation device, which emphasizes behavior as opposed to psychology, can be applied to this question. Chaikin set up a transformation improvisation about a trial.

THE TRIAL

There was a judge, a defendant, a prosecutor and a sympathizer, each occupying a different corner of an imaginary square. Each actor searched for the sounds, movements, and gestures which captured the essence of his social role. Dialogue was not important, nor were the circumstances of a particular case. Of significance were the five or six elements of physical expression which captured the attitude behind judging, defending or whatever. Then at a signal, each actor moved out of his corner and went along one side of the square toward the next corner. As he went, he gradually dropped his behavior as, say, the judge and adopted the behavior of, say, the defendant. At first he picked up the sounds and movements of the actor preceding him, but once in the new corner he made them his own. Thus the actors transformed from one (social) role to another, but *gradually* rather than instantaneously. The improvisation confirmed the interdependence of the parts in a situation, showing that the judge exists only because the defendant exists. The judge and the defendant address themselves not to different things, but to the same thing from different angles. Because of the difference in their social roles, the same thing (the event of the trial) which makes the judge firm and confident, makes the defendant shy and inhibited. The improvisation showed the arc of the actor's transformation from role to role, a visualization of the fact that anybody can be anybody, provided he drops one mode of behavior and assumes another. This was a dramatic visualization of an aspect of real life which naturalism obscures due to its reliance on psychology as the source for character.

∞

"THE CONTEST"

"The Contest" was developed improvisationally to show how men allow themselves to be controlled. The company of actors lined up under the command of two or three "guards," who prevented them from jumping place, pushing, shoving, and sent people caught at it to the end of the line. Facing the line was someone laughing, and the actor at the head of the line went forward to try to make him stop. He used any means he could devise. If he couldn't do it, he went to the end of the line, and the next person took a try. If he succeeded, he replaced the person laughing.

This was a strange piece. It was enjoyable because of the infectiousness of the laughter on stage, because of the *outré* things which the contestants did in order to succeed. But just behind that behavior were some ugly facts: the arbitrariness of rules, the foolishness of the ambition, the subordination of all aspirations to this trivial goal.

∞

Besides the inquiry into social behavior, Chaikin's workshop moved on another front. This was a broad inquiry into man's inner experience.

> From Chaikin's notebooks:
>
> We are born little animals unable to care for ourselves and crying with anger at being alive. Our voice becomes

> what is necessary for talking English. Our wishes are modified by what it is possible to attain. The whole spectrum of our imagination humbles itself to what is available to our understanding—except in science and art. . . . I am unwilling to be bored, charmed for nothing, taken in by that portrait of the established called truth, which receives all the garbage of history as an inheritance to accept without question. There are other states and other relationships, to which we can be transported—through music, drugs, sex, mysticism, dreams, hallucinations. . . . Perchance to dream—a chance to dream—that is the idea, and that is the poetic notion—to dream about that which exists besides that which there is. . . . Acting is the simple testimony that we can be other than what we are.

Other states and other relationships, implicit in the kinetic release of such techniques as the inside-outside, the conductor exercises, and the sound-and-movement vocabulary itself, became the subject of some specific improvisations.

"THE ILLUSION SCENE"
"The Illusion Scene" made use of a spatial adjustment in order to establish visually the relationship among three distinct states of being. Three concentric circles were drawn on the workshop floor. The outermost ring represented real life; the next ring was an area of passage; the inner circle stood for illusion, or utopia. The actors moved around in the outer ring, using sounds and movements expressive of lament, which was the designated mode of behavior there. They could move into the next ring at any time, and there they could make use of any vocabulary, including conventional speech; however, horror was the life-mode there. In the innermost circle, the actors sought to express peace and communion. But they could not enter this area at will. Someone

already there had to rescue them from horror or lament, and bring them in, and to do this he had to pass through horror himself. Chaikin thought that the work failed to find an effective dramatic expression of the ideal state of being, but he considered "The Illusion Scene" an important démarche into a difficult area—"an organic graft of a moment of living and dreaming extended on the stage."

∞

"Picnic in Spring," a playlet of van Itallie's, was related to this work. It was about the realization of the end of loving. Several couples went on a picnic in the woods. The action was naturalistic until, midway through a game of catch, things became abstract. The actors imagined that the woods were expanding, and that everything was getting farther and farther away from everything else. They called brief statements of isolation and despair to each other as if over a great distance ("where are you?"; "I am alone"; "forgive me"). They moved into the spatial adjustment of the circles, where they improvised on indifference, dread, and illusion, retaining the called phrases as the only speech. The use of the circles format isolated the states of being which were the components of the situation and made them visible. (Incidentally, van Itallie called the abstract section of this playlet the inside of the naturalistic section.)

WORLDS

Another investigation of inner experience is an ensemble improvisation known as worlds. Using sound-and-movement, a single actor improvises a particular inner state— paranoia, narcissism, dread, euphoria. This is his world, and other actors enter it by participating in his improvisation. They can parallel his action, set it in relief, flesh out a detail, and so on, but they must enter into his world, not transform it.

The actor beginning the improvisation works on himself. But the others try to participate in something alien to themselves. Thus they open themselves up to experiencing an unknown state of being. As in all ensemble playing, the actors work off what they find around themselves.

∞

In Chaikin's workshop, the worlds work was an attempt to understand states of being outside each person's own experience. Chaikin has tried to have each member of the group establish a world. Thus each can show the others a special place of his own, and, in the course of the improvisation, admit others to that place. The approach has furthered the cohesiveness of the troupe.

A few playlets were related to worlds. The character of the fool, with which the workshop concerned itself for a time, came out of group discussions about utopia. The fool was the ideal creature, in the sense that he was not civilized. He had no memory and was incapable of learning anything. Permanently innocent, he lived in awe of everything and was completely available to whatever he encountered. He was an amoral being, as capable of killing as of loving.

The scenario, "The First Fool," was one of a projected series about this character. The fool awoke in a cave, went outside into the woods, and encountered everything. The other actors helped articulate his world by embodying aspects of the environment. A second installment, "Simple Simon Meets the Pieman," put the fool into a social, i.e., commercial, situation in order to contrast the uncivilized with the civilized. But this episode was not finished, nor, as far as I know, performed, and the workshop abandoned the fool to take up other matters.

"The First Fool" and "Simple Simon" were improvisational playlets which van Itallie developed with the troupe; that is, they were fixed structures within which the actors improvised. Another playlet related to the fool was fully scripted, however. This is van Itallie's *The Hunter and the Bird*, a fantasy for an actor and an actress. The bird, who is shot down by the hunter at the beginning of the play, is like the fool. She is completely at home with whatever happens, whether she is flying in the sunshine or being wounded by the hunter. She loves the hunter because he is quite simply there to be loved; he is part of what is. The hunter, however, sees the bird as an object for use—he wants to learn the secret of flying from her. He is civilized. That is the simple point of the play. There is an ironical twist, however. As the hunter is preparing to leave, the bird asks to see his gun. When he obliges she shoots him dead and flies away. This transformation of roles (roles as life functions) is the logical extension of what the hunter had initiated; he has corrupted the bird, and he suffers the consequence.

"The Worlds of Rip Van Winkle" was another of the Open Theatre's improvisational playlets based on the worlds work. The legendary character revealed himself as a henpecked husband and went to sleep. He dreamed some political things about the Civil War, and then twenty years passed, and he woke up. He wandered through several worlds which actors created in different parts of the stage and tried to inhabit each of them. The natives of each world saw it as total and exclusive, but to Rip Van Winkle it was but one of several choices. As an outsider he saw each world as a framework for living, or the expression of one possible attitude. The point of view of the playlet—that the seemingly fixed structure of our living is in fact the result of our choice

—is a theme which the workshop has explored on several occasions.

Chaikin's workshops were observed from time to time by friends of the actors. On such occasions, the troupe did not so much perform as permit itself to be overseen and overheard. The response was generally enthusiastic, according to Gordon Rogoff, who had been attending regularly.

> At the time, Joe's work was developing along the lines of anybody-can-do-it, given a certain training or background and care about the material or the general thrust of that particular month. That's one of the qualities which made it so attractive—that it could come out of anybody at any time. We didn't know it then, but what we were doing was demonstrating that to be theatrical is to be alive, and to be alive, therefore, is to be theatrical.

Rogoff urged the idea of performing publicly, maintaining that a two-hour collection of Chaikin's improvisations and exercises would be a more entertaining theatre event than most of what was happening on the New York stage. Chaikin was reluctant, but enough members of the workshop favored the move, and it was made. The Open Theatre hired the Sheridan Square Theatre for two performances in December 1963 and the Martinique Theatre for two performances the following April. The program for the former performances carried the following explanation:

> What you will see tonight is a phase of work of the Open Theatre. This group of actors, musicians, playwrights, and directors has come together out of a dissatisfaction with the established trend of the contemporary theatre. It is seeking a theatre for today. It is now exploring cer-

tain specific aspects of the stage, not as a production group, but as a group trying to find its own voice. Statable tenets of this workshop: (1) to create a situation in which the actors can play together with a sensitivity to one another required of an ensemble, (2) to explore the specific powers that only the live theatre possesses, (3) to concentrate on a theatre of abstraction and illusion (as opposed to a theatre of behavioral or psychological motivation), (4) to discover ways in which the artist can find his expression without money as the determining factor.

The program opened with a sound-and-movement exercise, billed as "A Ritual Hello," which served to warm up the actors as an ensemble and to introduce the troupe *qua* troupe. (This became a standard feature of Open Theatre improvisational performances.) There were three improvisations. The title, "A Man Sometimes Turns into the Machine He Is Using," indicates what was made of a machines improvisation. A perfect people improvisation was done in the cocktail party format already described. A dream improvisation, a variety of the conductor exercise, was also done: the conductor lay on the floor as the dreamer and made slight motions and sounds, from which other actors conjectured the manifest content of his dream and expressed it in sound-and-movement.

There were two playlets for which van Itallie had supplied a structure and text. The first was "The Odets Kitchen" in an earlier version than the one already discussed entitled "Variation on a Clifford Odets Theme." The other was "An Airplane: Its Passengers and Its Portent."

This piece began with the actors forming the wings, propeller, and tail of the plane, and taking off. Then they transformed into passengers, a stewardess, a pilot, and co-pilot. The passengers were character types: the German businessman and the English countess in presidential deluxe class; the rich American bridge-playing lady and the teenage girl in first class; the American brat and her German grandmother in economy class. Each couple had a comic scene with the stewardess, who did the standard coffee-tea-or-milk routines. In the cockpit, it developed that the pilot was incompetent, and things began to get out of hand. The actors used the focus technique to shift back and forth from the cockpit to the passenger sections. As things became worse, the pilot went to the rear of the plane, ostensibly to use the toilet, and parachuted out of the rear door. At that point, the tone of the play began a progressive transformation from comic to grave. The co-pilot tried to control the plane; the stewardess tried to calm the frightened passengers. Again, each pair of passengers had a brief scene—this time showing the ways in which people react to the realization of imminent death. The plane began to go down. The actor who had played the pilot came back on stage in a death mask and embodied the plane hurtling to the ground. The others transformed from passengers into parts of the plane fragmenting during the fall. (In this, the ex-stewardess was the catalyst, cueing the other actors.) At the crash, the ex-pilot removed the death mask and came down to the front of the stage; the other actors joined him and stared as the dead at the audience.

The playlet is interesting for its use of several technical devices which the Open Theatre had developed in workshop—machines, focus, transformation, catalyst, sound-and-movement. Furthermore, as a metaphor for mortality, "The Airplane" articulated a concern which would continue to preoccupy the workshop: in evolving the comedy and satire of the first section into the grim disaster of the second, the piece showed people moving from security and triviality to danger and vulnerability.

The last work on the program, *Eat at Joe's*, a scripted playlet by Miss Terry which Sydney Schubert Walter directed, had the distinction of being the first of the transformation plays. In the workshop Miss Terry had seen that the actors tended to grab for clichés under the pressure of improvising transformations. She wrote this play in order to give them security and free them to act. She was amazed to see them use it in performance, however, as a base for improvisation. The Open Theatre has always had a tendency to keep its work open to the inspiration of the moment. Miss Terry's chagrin about it is one pole of a tension which is characteristic of the writer's relationship with the workshop. *Eat at Joe's* was a minuscule play, and the quarrel was a minor one, but it is noteworthy that the matter came up in connection with the Open Theatre's first original script.

The next April, at the Martinique, the troupe identified itself for the first time as the-Open-Theatre-under-the-direction-of-Joseph-Chaikin. Fourteen actors were listed as the permanent company, Miss Terry, Smith, and van Itallie as playwright members—with van Itallie getting a separate mention as "Playwright of the Workshop"—Feldman, Syd Walter, and Ira Zuckerman as directors, and Gordon Rogoff as adviser.

The usual sound-and-movement improvisation came first. There were a taboo improvisation called "Party and Dream," "The Contest," and van Itallie's "Picnic in Spring." After two short plays which I will discuss separately, the program ended with an innocent item called "Some Singing by the Actors," which was a singing transformation intended to give the evening an up ending.

The Clown Play is part of Brecht's *A Lesson in Understanding*. The Open Theatre has performed it each season since 1963–64 as a signature piece. It is a routine for three circus clowns, of whom the principal is Mr. Smith and the others are his sycophants. When Mr. Smith complains that his foot is tired, his friends offer to make it feel better; they do this by sawing it off. When pains turn up in his other leg and his hand, they help him similarly. When he complains of hearing unpleasant things, they remove his ear, and when he tells them about his unhappy thoughts, they de-brain him. The sycophants make each operation a feat of great moment through the particular razz-a-ma-tazz characteristic of clowns. The result of their elaborate concern is that Mr. Smith lies in a heap on the floor, for which Brecht's tag line is "Come to the clown play and see how man helps man."

The other Martinique play was a chilling, topical work by van Itallie inspired by the murder of Kitty Genovese, of whose misfortune the *New York Times* had made a *cause célèbre*, because of the heartlessness of her neighbors beneath whose windows she was raped and killed. In *The Murdered Woman*, four domestic scenes occurred at the same time, and the focus shifted among them. In one of the scenes an argument broke out between a man and his girlfriend, and he attacked her with a knife. She fled into the other scenes, where, according to the quality of life which had been developed there, she was ignored or rejected. She died unheeded, and the play ended with a coda of lines taken from the preceding action.

The performances at the Sheridan Square and the Martinique were more like open workshops than finished productions, and the audience was part of a coterie. Yet from the experience the Open Theatre gained a sense of its own identity, which contributed to getting the troupe established. Another event which contributed to the troupe's emerging sense of itself as an entity was the apparent demise of the Living Theatre, whose premises had been seized by Treasury agents the previous October.

The Becks, according to Chaikin himself, have had the most profound influence on him of anyone. In 1967 he told me that he couldn't imagine what he would be like or what he would be thinking about if he hadn't worked with them. They led him to Brecht, to Artaud, and the poetic drama. They opened up his political and social conscience. They impressed him with their fanatical commitment to their work. They set him a model for the communal structure of theatre work and for the confrontation of one's life with the values which emerge from one's work. Their respect for persons and disrespect for institutions are in Chaikin, as well as their spirit of self-criticism. He is struck, as he wrote of them (*Village Voice*, October 17, 1968), by their demonstration "in their work and in their activism that there are almost no boundaries; that no one need stay within the limitations which seem to be fixed. They represent a repudiation of the captive way of life. That is their spectacle."

Through Chaikin, Feldman, Lee Worley, and a few others who had worked with the Becks, the Open Theatre stood in filial relationship to the Living Theatre. Thus when that troupe seemed to be defeated, the Open Theatre experienced the difcult but salutary sensation of being on its own.

The beginning and end of "Sunday Morning," an unnoticed action improvisation.

Richard Bellak

James Barbosa as Mr. Smith is offered help in his distress by Seth Allen in the Angry Arts presentation of Brecht's *Clown Play*.

Phill Niblock/Martin Bough

Mr. Smith receiving help from his companions.

Richard Bellak

Sharon Gans, Isabelle Blau and Cynthia Harris in Megan Terry's *Calm Down Mother*.

Phill Niblock

James Barbosa, Ron Faber and Joseph Chaikin in two transformations in Miss Terry's *Keep Tightly Closed in a Cool Dry Place*.

Phill Niblock

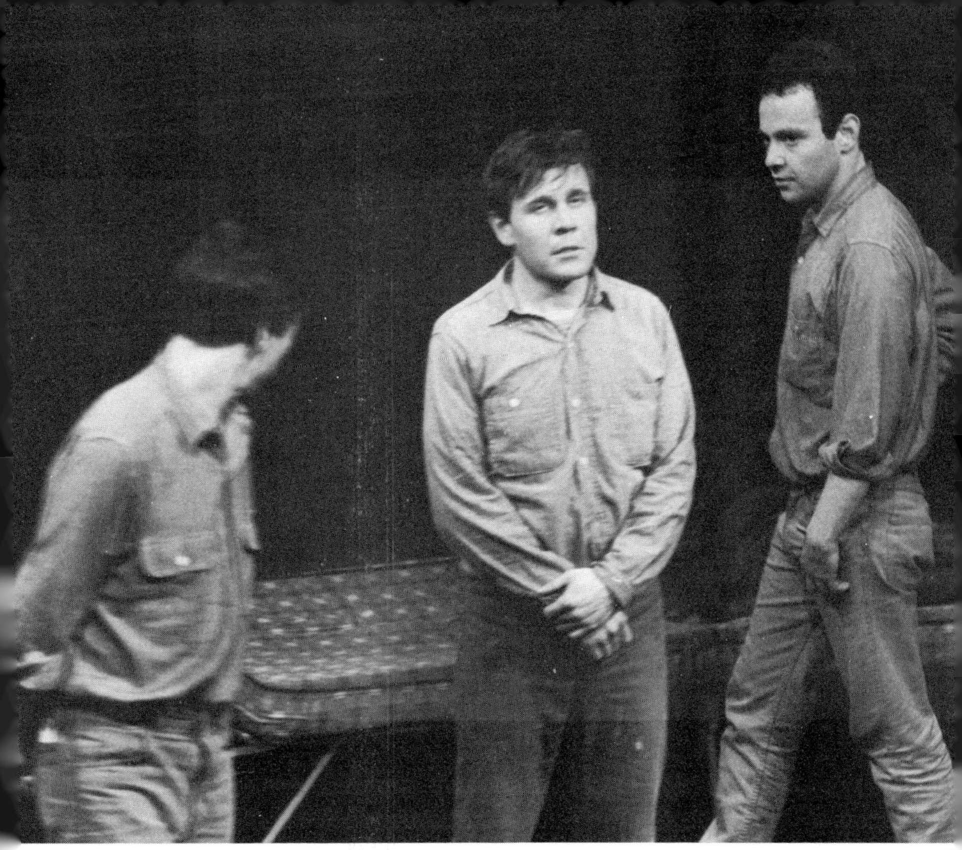

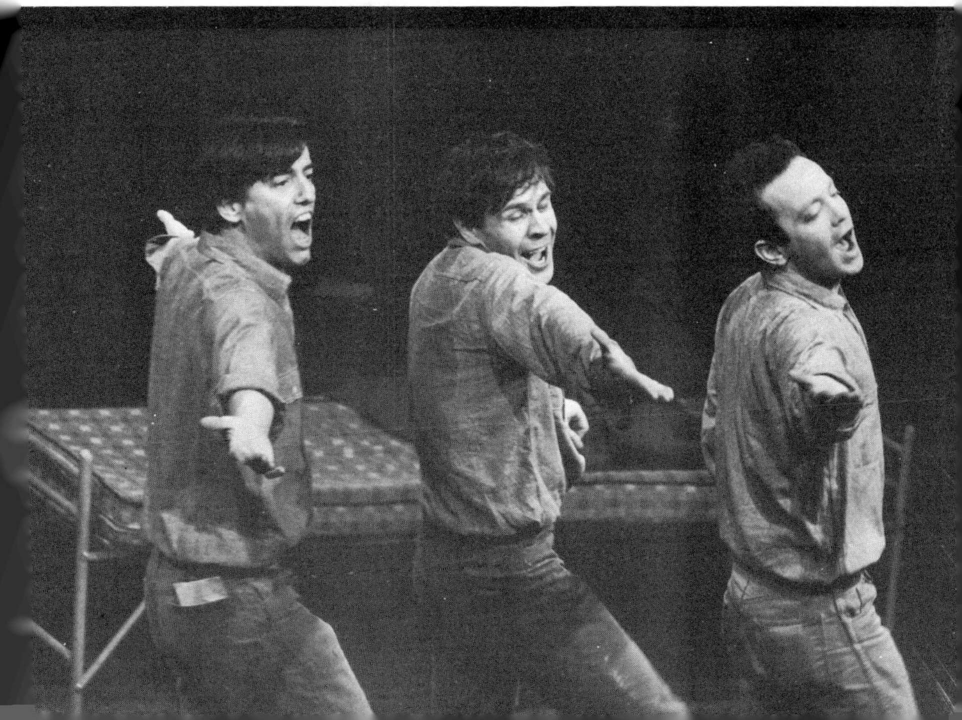

A war-machine in Miss Terry's *Viet Rock* off-Broadway.
    Henry Grossman/ Transworld Feature Syndicate, Inc.

Rebirth after the final scene of *Viet Rock* at the Cafe La MaMa.
    Phill Niblock

The Subway Scene in Jean-Claude van Itallie's *Interview* off-Broadway. The two actors at the top, Conard Fowkes and Cynthia Harris, impersonate a subway ad.
Phill Niblock/ Martin Bough

The final scene in van Itallie's *TV*.
Phill Niblock/ Martin Bough

Peter Maloney does a shoulder stand and Jayne Haynes a head stand. *Hope Wurmfeld*

Chaikin and the actors—the Bible workshop. *Richard Bellak.*

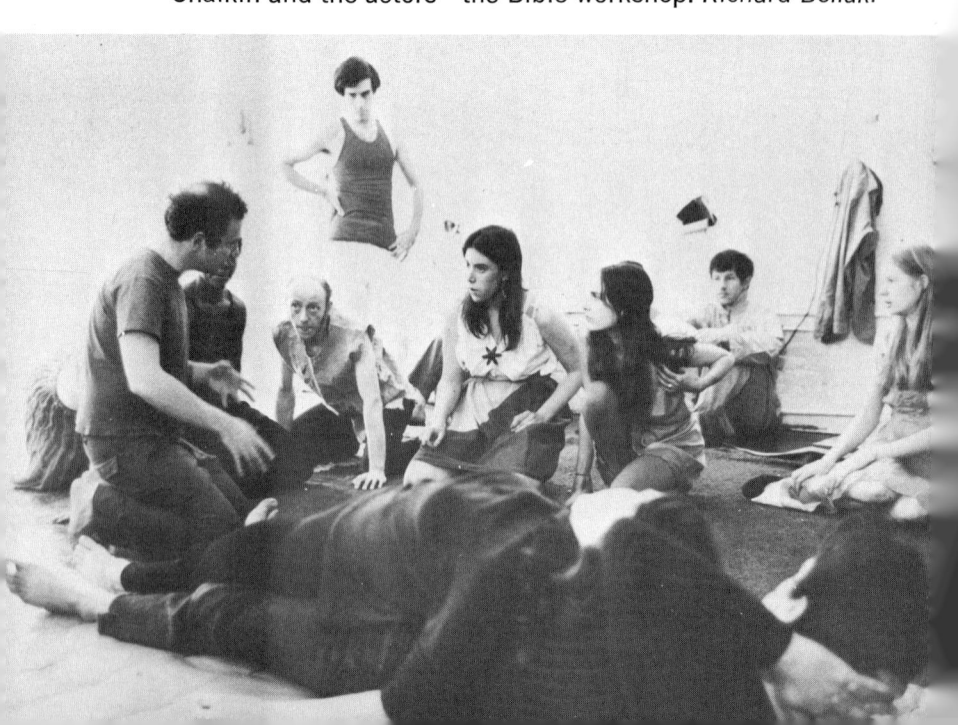

The Bible workshop.
Phill Niblock

The Bible workshop: Adam (Philip Harris) accuses Eve, who accuses the serpent.
Phill Niblock

The creation of Eve in *The Serpent:* Tina Shepard and Philip Harris. The other actors are imaginary animals of the Garden of Eden.

Richard Bellak

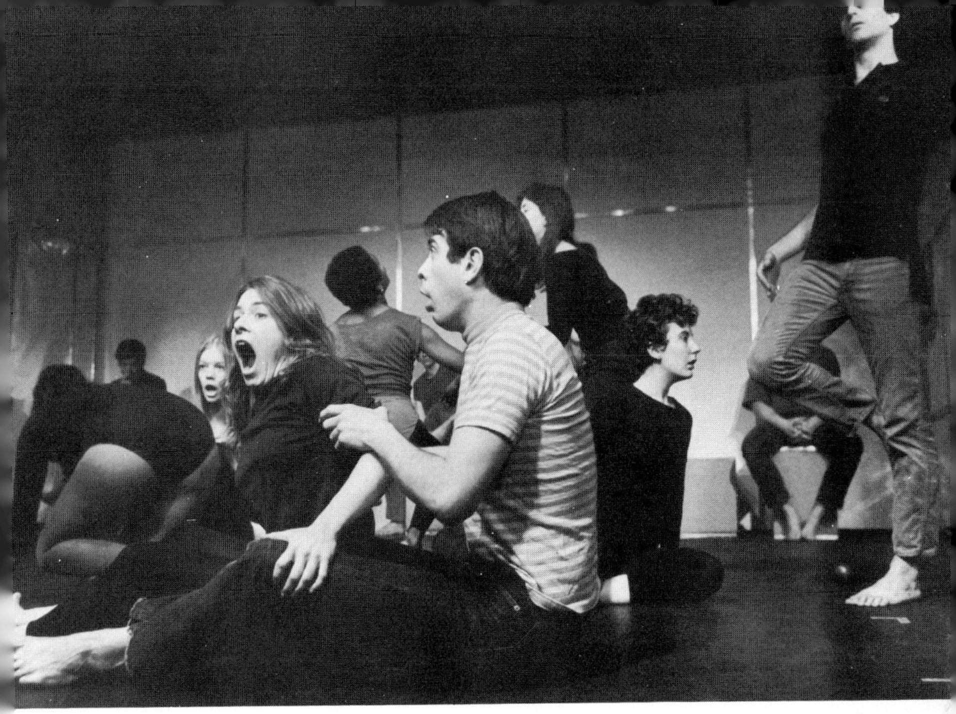

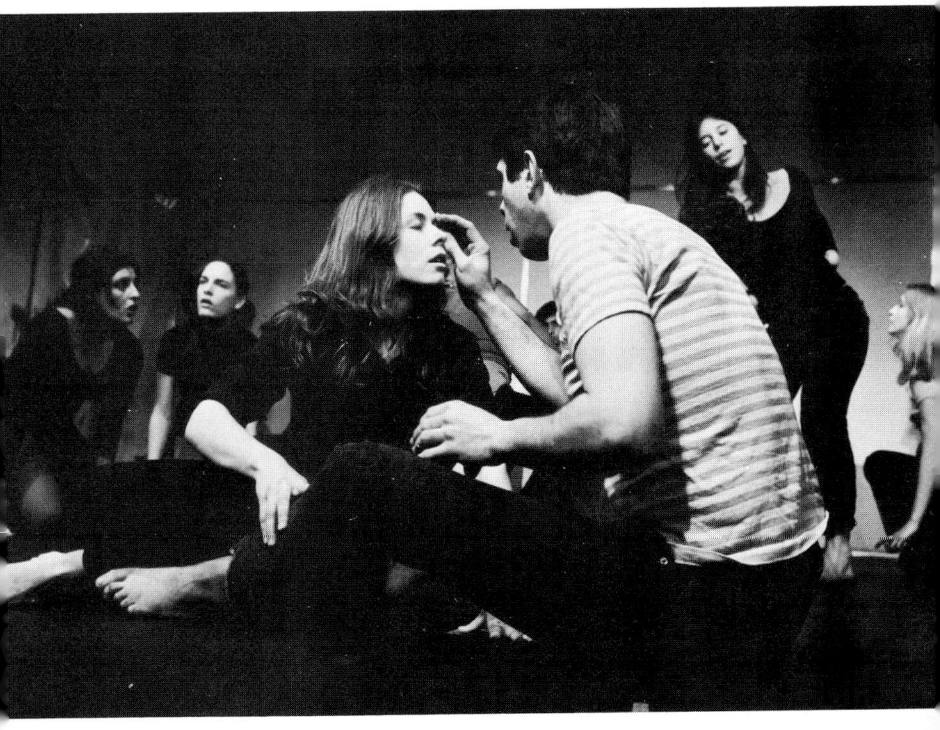

Eve and the serpent eat the apple. The serpent was played by five actors: Ralph Lee, Peter Maloney, Ron Faber, James

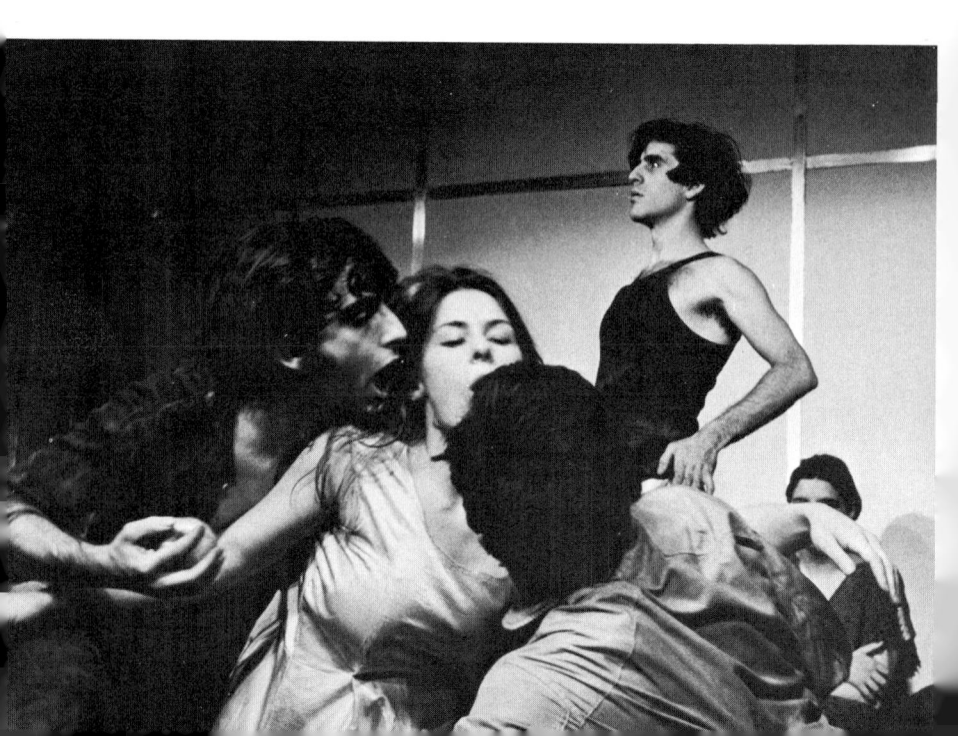

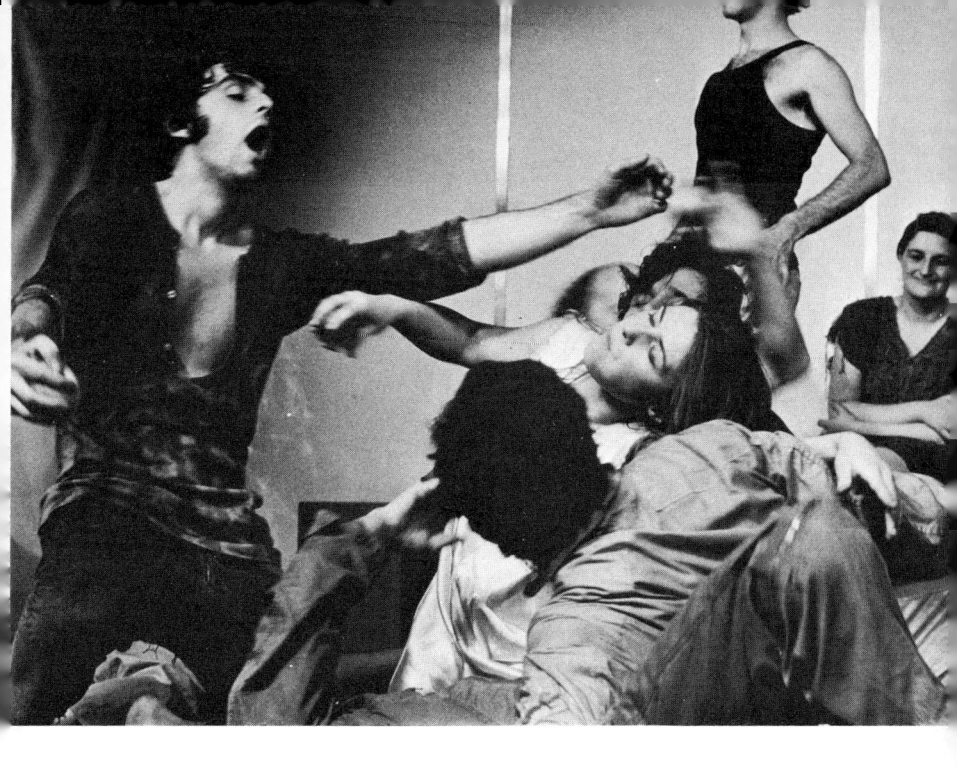

Barbosa and Raymond Barry. The heron, played by Paul Zimet, is behind them. *Hope Wurmfeld*

The Kennedy-King-Kennedy killing in *The Serpent*.

Karl Bissinger

God's curses in *The Serpent*.

Karl Bissinger

The company serpent at the end of the play.

Karl Bissinger

EXPANSION AND STRUGGLE 4

Peter Feldman was a close friend of Chaikin's who had shared a dressing room with him at the Living Theatre, where he had worked primarily as an assistant director. Feldman had also studied with Nola Chilton and knew the group of her actors who organized the Open Theatre with Chaikin; he was, in fact, one of the founding members. But it was not until the 1963–64 season that he became active. Having observed Chaikin's workshop for some time, he started his own in order to try out some of the exercises and improvisations which were being developed. He worked with actors who could not find places in Chaikin's workshop and with others whom he had known from his outside projects. He has continued to run workshops from time to time over the years.

Feldman is not an innovator like Chaikin. His gift as a workshop leader is in the area of training; he is sensitive to the place which an actor has reached in his development and creative in finding ways to extend it. Feldman makes use of the Spolin exercises and of Michael Chekhov's principles of the radiant center of energy and physical adjustments in exercises designed to build the actor's awareness. The following exercises figure prominently in his workshops.

SPHERE OF AIR
As the actor walks around the work area he imagines that there is a sphere of air around him which is growing larger and larger. He grows with it—expanding and lengthening until he occupies the largest possible space, one which embraces everything and everybody in the area. Then he imagines the reverse, that the sphere of air is contracting and himself with it, until he occupies the tiniest possible space, curled up, shrivelled, and shrunken.

∞

RADIATING ENERGY

Moving freely in the work area, the actor imagines that he has an energy source in the middle of his chest sending energy out in all directions—to his head, his hair, his eyes, his limbs, his buttocks. He imagines that the center of energy controls every part of him and is responsible for his movement and life. He tells himself that the energy gives him great power and will never fail him. Then he imagines that the center of energy is located elsewhere in the body, e.g., the tip of the nose, or outside the body, e.g., six inches from the back. Usually the actor thinks of the energy source as a radiating sun. Now he is asked to change it to a hard lump of coal or a blob of marshmallow. Still, however, it supplies the energy which is his life.

∞

MOLDING THE AIR

The actors pair off and apply their energy to a shared sphere of air. They move it around and give it shape, exerting force with various parts of the body, not just the hands. Still in pairs, they choose an ordinary household action, such as setting the table or making the bed, and they pour their energy into it.

∞

BODY MOLDING

Here the group divides into trios. One of each trio is regarded as a shapeless lump of clay. The other two give him human shape by making molding motions as close to his body as possible without touching him. They form his trunk, arms, legs, facial features, etc. Secondly, they give him action. They imagine that energy radiates from their centers through their arms and hands, and they impart it to the subject, thus giving him life. The two actors work together but without conferring; they communicate within the doing. The

EXPANSION AND STRUGGLE / 59

subject's job is to sense the passage of energy and to bring the parts of his body to life accordingly.

∞

SENSE ADJUSTMENT

This is an Actors Studio exercise which starts with two or three actors improvising a simple story. Then the workshop leader makes suggestions for physical adjustments ("you're about to throw up," "your left leg is shrinking"). Using the original improvisation as text, the actors run through it again taking the physical adjustments into account. Then the leader makes place adjustments ("you're on the beach," "you're in the men's room at Grand Central Station"). The actors repeat the scene. Finally, the actors decide on a piece of "secret information" (one of their wives has just had a baby boy). When the improvisation is done again, the secret information is not introduced into the action, but is allowed to influence how the scene is done.

∞

The imperatives of actors training in the basic skills within Feldman's workshop are indicative of his larger place within the Open Theatre. His penetrating and orderly mind, his tenacity in thinking things through, his ability to conceptualize in matters of aesthetics and theatrical principles have been extremely important to a group dominated by Chaikin's impulsive and inspirational mode of work. Feldman is a person of calm and constancy who has contributed greatly to what continuity the Open Theatre has had, which is relevant not only to Feldman's relationship to the troupe, but, crucially, to his friendship with Chaikin, who has had other confreres and "voices" but none so loyal as Feldman. Feldman has been an invisible stabilizer within the Open Theatre.

Richard Gilman came to the Open Theatre in the spring of 1964. Chaikin's workshop seemed to him like an oasis within the theatre. He thought that the troupe was on the track of something enormously important, but that the work was not purposeful enough. And he was dismayed by the emphasis on private pursuits as a kind of personal therapy. His role at the workshops, which he attended frequently for the next year, became what Chaikin describes for both Gilman and Rogoff as an "instructor in perspective." He tried to awaken the group to the need to define its artistic goals more precisely and to consolidate its energies toward reaching them. He gave talks on theatre history, movements in the other arts, and contemporary thought. He tried to piece together an intellectual framework within which it would be possible for the Open Theatre to locate its work.

Gilman took a stand against the amateur spirit, which some members championed as a vital corrective to the dehumanization of the professional theatre. Gilman urged professionalism on the troupe, calling attention to the root sense of the word: to stand forth and assume the full consequence of what you do. He operated as a counter-force to many of Chaikin's natural inclinations. For example, he urged the troupe to perform publicly on a regular basis. And after the summer of 1964, which a portion of the company spent in relaxed work and communal living at van Itallie's isolated farm house in the Berkshires, Gilman's point of view was adopted. The troupe rented its own loft in the downtown manufacturing district of Manhattan, and set to work vigorously to prepare several programs. These were shown publicly in an ambitious series at the Sheridan Square: eight programs on alternate Monday nights from February to May, 1965.

There were ten plays, ten improvisations and five pre-set improvisations. Plays first: Brecht's *Clown Play*, and van Itallie's *The Hunter and the Bird* I have already discussed. There were T. S. Eliot's *Sweeney Agonistes*, directed by Barbara Vann, and John Arden and Margaretta D'Arcy's *Ars Longa Vita Brevis*, directed by Harvey Cort. There was also Feldman's superb production of *Pavane*, the play which van Itallie rewrote as *Interview*, part of *America Hurrah*.

Two other van Itallie plays came out of the group's investigation of social roles. There were "the Doris plays"—*It's Almost Like Being* and *I'm Really Here*. (The former was done in the Sheridan Square season. The latter had been done in August as part of a benefit performance, and both were done at the Playwrights Unit of Theatre 1965 in February.) The group had earlier worked on a scene called "Betty," intended as an inflight movie to be "shown" during "The Airplane," but it was not used. "Betty" was a parody of the Joan Crawford movies, in which a small-town girl yielded to her yen for the big city, where she fell into disillusionment and degradation until her former home-town sweetheart found her in a Times Square dive, rekindled the pure flame in her heart, took her back to the old home town, where he was the pastor, and helped her find new wisdom, happiness, etc., etc.

The Doris plays make use of the clichés of the Doris Day–Rock Hudson movies of the early 1960's and capture the Hollywood formula in a manner both incisive and novel. The satire of movie formula is itself a formula by now, but the Doris plays do it afresh, partly because of van Itallie's production device:

> This play is to be done as if it were a movie being shot by several cameras. When the individual actors are not,

for a moment or two, on camera, their expression is deadpan and bored. They are "turned on" for their "bits." Often Doris will make a facial expression especially for the camera, or she will address it instead of another actor. The actors will always know exactly where the camera is at a given moment—sometimes a closeup, sometimes a two-shot, panning, etc. This technical device should serve as a comment on the action.

The cutting edge of the performance device is an analogue to the sharp wit of the lines and situations: the plays seem close to the definitive satire on Hollywood.

I want to call attention to the final scene of *I'm Really Here*. The scene begins with a startling split of the play into two levels: on the literal level the scene is a murder—Rossano teases Doris with a knife and then stabs her; on the metaphorical level it is a love scene—Rossano deflowers the reluctant Doris. (Part of the richness of the scene is that the previous events of the play had led up to a love scene, not to a murder: that which had been literal becomes metaphorical.) Then Rossano stabs (rapes) Doris and walks out:

> Rossano (leaving). Au revoir, Miss Prettyasabutton. This time, c'est la vie.

> Doris (on the floor, in increasing fear). But the other man, the nice one, is coming to save me. I'm always saved. Someone will come. I'll be all right. Everything's coming up roses, Doris. Doris. Doris, take hold of yourself. I'm going to wash that man right out of my hair. I'm going to—I'm alone. Doris. Some enchanted evening you will see? meet? see? a stranger. But I'm Doris. I love Paris in the springtime

when it drizzles. Doris. I'm alone. Help me. Forgive me. I'm alone. I can't die. Doris can't die. Die? Die? I'm dying. *I am dying. Really dying.* I'm really—.

(She screams loudly in fear. Curtain.)

Suitably, the scene is played, according to the stage directions, "as if the cameras were locked in place. Doris could not get out of this movie now if she wanted to." This is the same irony which occurred in "The Airplane": the imminence of death awakens Doris, finally, to real life.

The Doris plays were written at a time when pop art was the rage. Today people tend to dismiss them as if their source in popular culture, their hard-edge, their two-dimensionality of character disqualify where once they had qualified. Van Itallie himself is no longer interested in the parody of the Doris plays, while Chaikin regards all of the Open Theatre's satirical work as a temporary aberration. Although I appreciate the importance of this growing seriousness of purpose, I do think that the Doris plays have a more lasting significance, especially *I'm Really Here*.

Another of the Sheridan Square plays was *The Successful Life of Three, a skit for vaudeville,* by Maria Irene Fornes. The characters of this play are two-dimensional characterizations. Named He, She, and Three, they live in a ménage à trois. He is a fall guy; She is a dumb broad; Three is an operator. Their lives have little significance: they do things; things happen; they react. The activity of their lives engages them, but not its meaning. The reason for this is that they have no emotional life whatsoever; they are feelingless freaks.

The vaudeville structure of the action makes a counterpoint to this inanity. A series of double takes, non sequiturs, freezes and blackouts makes the three characters quite charming and the play witty and funny. The play is descriptive, with a comment on the description. It is the most phenomenological approach to character that I know of. The vaudeville is not an acting style which the actors use, but a style of life which imbues the characters' being. A member of the audience remarked that the play was like a comic strip, and I agree. It is great fun, but its implications are chilling. Although it is founded on a deeply pessimistic observation of the way we live our lives, it refuses not to be gay. Richard Gilman's brightly colored, brisk production was a tour-de-force.

Meg Terry contributed two transformation plays to the season, one for women called *Calm Down Mother*, the other for men, called *Keep Tightly Closed in a Cool Dry Place*. Unlike her short transformation script *Eat at Joe's* which was an exercise for the actors, these plays used transformations to illuminate matters of concern to Miss Terry.

In a sequence of ten short scenes, *Calm Down Mother* explores the relationships of mothers, sisters, and daughters. The characters and abstract characterizations change from scene to scene, but the same three actresses use the transformation device to do them all. As the characters change, so do the relationships between them, the locales, the dramatic actions, the tone of the scenes, the moods. There is no overall narrative; the unity of the play is its theme of female relationships. As in all transformation plays, exposition and transitions between scenes are ignored; *Calm Down Mother* covers a great deal in a short space; it is dramatically exciting, at times breathtakingly pyrotechnic.

Keep Tightly Closed in a Cool Dry Place is a more complex play. Here Miss Terry combines transformations of character with an overall dramatic situation and a narrative progression. She took the idea for the play from a newspaper item about three men who had been convicted of a murder and assigned to the same cell. She says that she wrote the play as a speculation on what their lives in the cell were like.

Jaspers is the dominant personality. He is a lawyer who hired Michaels to hire Gregory to murder his wife. The court has found them all guilty, but Jaspers hopes for a retrial at which one of the others will take the blame alone. First he tries to use Michaels to maneuver Gregory into signing a confession; then he tries to manipulate Michaels to sign. Neither scheme works, and at the end of the play it is clear that the three men will stay together in a prison defined as much by their characters and relationships as by the geographical situation.

Realistic scenes in the cell advance the plot, but interpolated scenes related to historical episodes, gangster movies, music-hall routines and church services flesh out the characters and relationships of the three men. Thus the scene transformations create not only a rich variety of incident, but an unusually dense presentation of character. Aspects of character and relationship which can only be implied or discussed in a conventional play are here made visible. The elementary maxim of the playwriting manuals—don't tell it, show it—is fully observed. Miss Terry accomplishes in an hour and a half what it would take a conventionally structured play five days to show.

The extraordinary dramaturgy of *Keep Tightly Closed* does not demand one specific production approach. Directors' notes from various productions show that different people make different sense of the play. One director picked up Miss Terry's note from the published text that "the three men can be seen as aspects of one personality" and made Jaspers the superego attempting to control the sensualist Gregory as the id through the mediation of Michaels as the ego. The great variety of incident released by the transformations makes *Keep Tightly Closed* a play to work with.

Peter Feldman directed the play at the Sheridan Square. Like most of Feldman's work, the production was carefully planned and controlled, which contributed to an impressive sense of confinement. I have seen the play done with great animation and vivacity, but Feldman's production made it a question of rats in a cage rather than monkeys.

Besides the ten scripted plays, the troupe presented five set improvisations. "The Airplane," "Rip Van Winkle," "The First Fool" and "The Contest" I have already discussed. The remaining one, called "Panel Show," was devised by Feldman in workshop. The name of the show was "Why Should You Live?" Contestants came on to justify their lives before a panel of dim-wits, which then decided whether the contestants should go on living. The point was in the irony of the contrast between the desperate circumstances detailed by the contestants and the empty, facile, superficial reactions of the panelists.

Among the improvisations performed by the troupe were open transformations, style transformations, singing transformations, unnoticed actions and the usual opening warm-up.

The public for the Sheridan Square season was a downtown public, but it was more heterogeneous than the collection of friends and relations which had been the audience for the open workshops of the previous season. This audience met the Sheridan Square programs with great enthusiasm. One reason was the verve and animation of the company, which seemed no less than miraculous.

Chaikin saw the performances as tools serving his workshop research, rather than the usual other way around. He told me that he considered the season a chance "to see where we were in problem solving; how far we had gotten, and what was left for us to do; these were insights which performing could give us." Typically, he found a way to make use of the Sheridan Square performances in his own concern with research. To Chaikin, outside opinion has always been a pressure to avoid. He considers success before the public to be as harmful to his work as failure, for both experiences inevitably coerce actors to modify their work and their working relationships. The expertise of an actor in performance which might delight the spectators and critics often disturbs Chaikin. The presentational solution, especially in its reliance on satire and comedy—that which Rogoff called "the leap to the audience"—seems to Chaikin too easy and too glib. In part this is a measurement of performance against the enormous possibilities in which the workshop deals. Also it measures performing against Chaikin's elemental notion of ensemble playing, which is easily disrupted by the presence of non-participants. Yet actors must eventually make the theatrical event, which involves spectators, or their workshop effort will collapse. Chaikin's tactical sanction of performance is an example of his diplomatic relationship to the affairs of the troupe.

At the time of the Sheridan Square season the Open Theatre comprised sixteen actors under Chaikin's direction, with

Feldman and Syd Walter as associate directors. There were four playwrights (Miss Fornes, Miss Terry, van Itallie, and Smith, with van Itallie listed as "Playwright of the Ensemble" as well), four stage directors (Harvey Cort, Rhea Gaisner, Ira Zuckerman, and Lynn Laredo), two advisers (Gilman and Rogoff), three administrative volunteers, and fifteen associate members, most of them actors. That is a total of forty-six.

The core of the company remained from the time of the first program in December 1963: eight of the sixteen actors, three of the four writers, one of the four directors, plus Chaikin and Feldman. From the founding days in the spring of 1963 remained five of the actors (Isabelle Blau, Gerome Ragni, Barbara Vann, Lee Worley, and Murray Paskin), plus Chaikin and Feldman, and two of the writers (Miss Terry and Michael Smith).

The season had been a strain on the troupe. The demands of mounting an essentially new program every two weeks were considerable for a theatre group which had to fit its workshops and rehearsals into the personal schedules of people who earned their living elsewhere. There were shortcuts, last minute cancellations, eleventh-hour rescues. There was dissension within the company: one bloc charged the other with overambition; the other charged the first with paralytic timidity.

The 1964–65 season was the climax of the Open Theatre's work in the bright-spirited, pyrotechnical vein. The troupe would now move away from parody, pop, and in Richard Schechner's phrase, "pure performance," toward deeper, less antic work. But first the troupe would flounder, when, not yet free of the old ways, it was not yet controlling the new ones.

EXPANSION AND STRUGGLE / 69

Several of the actors, directors, and writers of the company had worked at Ellen Stewart's Cafe La MaMa, as indeed they had at many of the off-off-Broadway theatres. For the season of 1965–66, Miss Stewart arranged for the troupe to appear at her theatre during one week of each month. Whatever the spirit in which the Open Theatre made the agreement, once into the season it seemed more of a responsibility than an opportunity. This was especially true for Chaikin, who had spent the summer in Europe and traveled with the Living Theatre, contact with which must have confirmed the dissatisfactions which he had sustained from the Sheridan Square season and rekindled his sense of purpose for his workshop. Yet now the troupe was committed to performing once a month at the La MaMa, and there was little time for workshop as distinct from rehearsals. After the initial presentation at the Cafe, an improvisational program in October, Chaikin stayed aloof from the season until the spring. He did run a workshop, but the attendance was sparse and the attainment minor.

Without a viable Chaikin workshop, the Open Theatre lacked cohesion. Instead of a theatre troupe working on a series of productions, it became in 1965–66 a nominal umbrella for individual productions of scripted plays, each of which involved only a handful of the actors at a time. Some of these projects were successful, some not, but until *Viet Rock*, in May, they were definitely not the work of a theatre troupe. (For the record: Feldman directed van Itallie's *Dream;* Tom Bissinger directed Miss Terry's *The Magic Realists;* John Coe directed Sharon Thie's *Soon Jack November;* and Jacques Levy directed Smith's *The Next Thing*.) Furthermore, the membership had diffused. Gilman and Rogoff had drifted away; Walter had gone to Minneapolis to run the Firehouse Theatre; some actors had withdrawn. New members, if old friends, stretched the thin fabric thinner. The plays of the La MaMa season were directed and performed by as many new members as old; few of the new members continued with the troupe beyond 1966.

In April, Chaikin directed the troupe's annual presentation of *The Clown Play*, and for the same program Feldman did Miss Terry's "theatre game," *Comings and Goings*. This production made one aware again of the Open Theatre as a company. *Comings and Goings* is a transformation play with two characters, He and She, who enter and depart a series of naturalistic and abstract situations exposing the variety of relationships between men and women. Miss Terry originally wrote the play as a virtuoso vehicle for two members of the company, Sharon Gans and Jordan Charney. But a production scheme which she and Feldman developed in rehearsal entailed using three actors to alternate as He and three actresses as She. This scheme, which Miss Terry has incorporated into the published script, harkened back to an experience which Feldman had had when he worked at the Living Theatre. The Becks had experimented with chance plays, notably Jackson Mac Low's *The Marrying Maiden*, the words of which were extracted from the *I Ching* by a chance process. What the actors said made no sense at all, and only the explanation that the play meant something as a metaphor for the mystery of living enabled Feldman to adjust to it at all. The production of *Comings and Goings* was an opportunity to infuse the rigidity of chance theatre with the freedom of actors' improvisation. At irregular intervals, an actor not otherwise involved spun a wheel of fortune on which the other actors' names were printed. When the needle came to rest, the designated actor's name was called, and he went into the action from the sidelines to replace the actor of the same sex who had been performing. Since this could happen at any moment during the play, it was necessary for the entire cast to know the entire play, and since replacements were made individually rather than in couples, there were several playing combinations. This play is great fun—Miss Terry calls it "a trampoline for actors and director." Audiences enjoy the display of technical prowess. But there is more to it than that. Seeing an actor take over from another in the middle of a scene reminds one of the universality behind the particularity of relationships. This is not at all beside the point.

One of Chaikin's techniques which contributes to the actor's ability to do plays like *Comings and Goings* is "stop-and-start."

STOP-AND-START

Inspired by the great economy of action of Georg Büchner's play *Woyzeck,* Chaikin devised stop-and-start as a practical way to structure a group-created play in which only the high points of an action are to be dramatized—either because the story line is familiar, making the links between climaxes superfluous, or because the events have a thematic or conceptual relationship rather than a narrative one. The actors sit on the sidelines in view of the audience as actors, not as characters. An actor rises alone or with others when his cue occurs, assumes his character on the instant, and begins his action. When he has finished, he drops his character and returns to the sidelines. In succeeding scenes he plays the same character or different ones, depending on the script.

Because the actor jumps from neutrality to dramatic fullness without developing his character, plays based on stop-and-start emphasize dramatic event and de-emphasize character. Even if the scenes are naturalistic, they have an autonomy which the character-bound naturalistic play structure cannot achieve. Stop-and-start uses the actor unabashedly as a tool to serve dramatic events.

In exercising stop-and-start the actor concentrates on developing his ability to go from zero to full in an instant. The Open Theatre has structured these exercises in two ways, both of them employing improvisation. The first structure sets a few actors to talking and moving around as themselves. One of them begins to improvise a scene, and the others enter into it. After the objective of the scene is reached someone drops his part, and all return to themselves. As soon as possible, someone starts another scene, preferably with a different situation and different characters. Again the other actors enter it immediately, and so on.

The second exercise structure duplicates the performance situation with the actors sitting on the sidelines. The high points of a story line or the facets of a theme which will be dramatized are understood in advance. The workshop leader calls on particular actors to improvise the first scene. They do it and return to their places. After a pause, others are designated to do the next scene, and so on. Sometimes actors are assigned to particular characters and thus participate more fully in the sequence of scenes. In this case, the actor must concentrate on the total action of which only the high points are being played out. Since stop-and-start sequences do not allow for working up to an emotion in the playing, the actor must do his emotional investment in his head on his own.

Like the transformation exercise, these exercises serve to restore the balance of an actor who has done a great deal of character improvisation; they tend to firm up any lackadaisical and non-discriminating quality in his work. (Stop-and-start is like transformations in the variety of actions an actor enters into from scene to scene, and also in the necessity he faces to attain full intensity fast. The principal difference, however, is that there is a dead break between the actions of stop-and-start.)

The stop-and-start technique has the advantage of keeping the actor alive to the whole piece, rather than just his role. While sitting on the sidelines, he must go forward with the action in his mind if he is to be ready for his next event. This is related to the Brechtian concern with the actor's commitment to the ideology of the drama which he helps unfold.

∞

The Open Theatre next presented one of its most provocative productions, *Viet Rock*. This was the first full-length play developed improvisationally by a writer and the troupe, and the first one to harness the energy of the early improvisational evenings. *Viet Rock* came out of the workshop which Megan Terry ran on Saturdays during 1965-66; it culminated both the achievement of the late spring and the discord and frustration of the season as a whole.

>From Miss Terry's notebooks:

Too many plays are written after studying other plays. Not enough plays are written out of an observation of character, society, and current world problems. The theatre world is very small, and it keeps looking inward. It better lift its head and take a look around it if it wishes to join this century. I have been more entertained by amateur theatricals in college dormitories put on by non-theatrical aspirants than by the most ambitious productions at the multi-million dollar theatrical building complexes. Why don't . . . directors go out and open their ears and their eyes. Why don't they watch television news. Did they see the films of the National Guard firing on Negro apartment houses in Chicago? Did they hear the cries of suspects apprehended and dragged to the paddywagons? Where are the plays on the terror and pressure surrounding how to get into a college of your choice? Where are the plays about the teach-ins, academic freedom, grading men who are subject to the draft if they don't get high enough marks? There is so much material around I wish I were quintuplets.

Miss Terry has a Brechtian concern with the curable ills of the time. It is a corollary, no doubt, that the forms which she has found for expressing her concern have made her plays as sprightly, if not as tough-minded, as Brecht's. In her Saturday workshop Miss Terry and the actors examined the Vietnam war. They discussed, abstracted and improvised newspaper clippings, television accounts, and first-hand observation of events in both the United States and Vietnam. The motives behind the violence were examined; patriotic rhetoric was taken apart; the feelings aroused by the events of the war were questioned. The troupe looked into the impulse of the individual toward aggression, hostility, and destructiveness, and tried to understand the fears and insecurities which trigger it. Gradually a pastiche of patriotic skits, scenes of warfare, and dramatic comments emerged. Miss Terry scripted some scenes, and it was decided to make *Viet Rock* one of the La MaMa productions. As usual, it was a rush. Chaikin came in to work on acting problems; Feldman on staging problems. Miss Terry concentrated on finishing the script. The troupe met daily during the three weeks prior to the scheduled opening on May 21st, which was Armed Forces Day.

Viet Rock is the most extended of the transformation plays. The scenes are related through their common subject of the war. But there is a loose chronological narrative also—a story of young American men inducted, trained, taken to Vietnam, made to fight, attacked and killed. In larger terms, to which the play makes specific reference, the narrative is that of birth to death and, in a coda, rebirth. *Viet Rock* is richer in incident than Miss Terry's other transformation plays. Where *Calm Down Mother* and *Keep Tightly Closed* are short plays for only three actors, *Viet Rock* is a full-length play for as many actors as a director "feels confident to work with," according to Miss Terry. The Open Theatre production of *Viet Rock* used thirteen to sixteen actors at various times.

Furthermore, the organization of *Viet Rock* around a subject does not require as tight a focus as that necessary for *Calm Down Mother* and *Keep Tightly Closed*. The structure of *Viet Rock* is very like that of a motion picture; at the end of one scene the play cuts to the next, and the narrative moves forward. This is the relevance of the play's subtitle—"a folk war movie"—and explains why many people compare transformations to the cinema structure. As a description of the *Viet Rock* style the movie analogy is correct, but it oversimplifies. It doesn't take into account the essential mechanism of the transformation—the fact that the spectator sees an actor assume several roles. In the traditional theatre, character mediates between the event and the spectator. But in plays like *Viet Rock*, character is seen to be dispensable, for the actors put it on and off many times in the course of the play. *Viet Rock* is done without sets, costumes, or props, except for some benches where the actors sit when they are not involved in a particular scene. We look at them as actors, then as actors-as-characters, then as actors again. The play is more theatrical than dramatic.

Viet Rock is rich in sentiment set off by satire and grim humor. In its first performances at the La MaMa, the play had a priceless feel. Something tentative about the new production, perhaps the unpolished surface—an element of the amateur, in the good sense—gave the effect of a work created and performed by people who were vitally concerned about the subject. You had the impression that you had gone to somebody's garage to see some plain people attempt to say something of great personal importance to them. Yet counter to the feel of the production, there was, and is, something too cool, detached, and lacking in emotional force at the center of Viet Rock. Near the end of the play, a chorus of the dead says: "Who needs me. Who needs this. Who needs war. Who needs this shit. I'm in the shit. Who needs me. Who. Who needs. Who needs. Who." Although this moment makes one effect among many, it characterizes the overall tone of the play, a kind of weary dismissal which tends to reduce even the passionate scenes to lip service.

Miss Terry has often stated that Viet Rock was not intended as an invective. "Our confusion and sense of shame created by the war" is what she says interested her in the workshop exploration and in the final script. Chaikin and Feldman as co-directors, however, pressed for an angrier attitude, and a tone of more dissident irony, inspired, no doubt, by Brecht's anti-war plays. They reworked Viet Rock in that direction during their rehearsals of the play after the first La MaMa run, in preparation for another week of performances there late in June. But Miss Terry heatedly rejected their changes when she saw them at dress rehearsal. She insisted that the tone of light irony and tenderness be retained. She took sole charge of the production and held on to it during the play's subsequent career.

She and the actors, one of whom, Roy London, became her assistant director, reworked and revised the production during the summer and fall, gradually ridding it of its amateur feel, and, to my mind, draining it of its humanity. The company achieved the best balance between competence and conviction in July, when it performed the play at Sundance, a small festival of avant garde music, theatre, and dance in Bucks County, Pennsylvania. While the play was more vivid, shapely, and theatrically sharp, the execution of its elaborate scenario still seemed slightly beyond the competence of the actors. Thus the production retained its feel of concern, while it became more effective in theatrical terms.

In September, the cast went to Yale for three weeks of rehearsal prior to performing *Viet Rock* as the opening production in the professional season which Robert Brustein initiated as the new Dean of the Drama School. During this period, the bitter humor was emphasized, the pace tightened, the song and dance redoubled, the improvisational edge of the production all but erased. In short, *Viet Rock* was transformed into a professional entertainment, although a serious one. It was spirited, sometimes dazzling, occasionally movingly tender; it was pyrotechnic and, to me, very impressive. But the personal quality of the production had been suppressed; *Viet Rock* had left the garage and entered the theatre.

By November, when the play opened off-Broadway at the Martinique Theatre, however, it had somehow gotten soggy, as if the hard polished surface acquired at Yale had partially melted. The peculiar topography of the Martinique imposed a new awkwardness on the production. Despite the fact that the seating area wraps three sides around the stage, the company seemed brutally separated from the audience in a way which even the proscenium stages at Sundance and Yale had not imposed.

Backstage at the Martinique was known to be a disaster area. The row during the La MaMa presentation had opened a rift which divided the troupe—roughly between those who thought, with Miss Terry, that the Open Theatre should welcome the opportunities offered by the outside theatre, and those who feared, with Chaikin, that ambitions in that direction would usurp the energies and break down the relationships of the workshop. Chaikin's refusal to be involved with *Viet Rock* after the La MaMa performances had made some of the actors sensitive about their own involvement, and had wounded Miss Terry, who was the first writer to make a finished text out of Chaikin's discoveries and techniques, and the first whose work had brought the Open Theatre actors the opportunity to be employed as Open Theatre actors. (Nor did the decision to keep the Open Theatre name off the Martinique presentation, an expedient adopted to allay the discord, seem decent to Miss Terry.) The production plans for Yale and the Martinique mangled the troupe, some of whom were to perform at Yale, but not off-Broadway, others of whom were dropped after La MaMa. The presence of Chaikin and Feldman at Yale, where they gave workshops with the *Viet Rock* cast for the students of the Drama School, was more than awkward; their point of view became immediate to the cast again and was disruptive. Chaikin, in fact, did not fully resign himself to not influencing *Viet Rock* in the matter of its tone until November, when he was immersed in preparing for the off-Broadway production of van Itallie's *America Hurrah*. Chaikin's willingness to work on that commercial production, incidentally, deepened the chagrin felt by the *Viet Rock* company.

EXPANSION AND STRUGGLE / 79

One can theorize that the discord contributed to the alterations which *Viet Rock* underwent. Professionalism, which set in at Yale, is among other things a means by which theatre people avoid personal involvement in the work and with each other. The demoralization which set in at the Martinique caused the actors to become alienated from even the professional life of their show. It need not be supposed that the difficulties surrounding the production of *Viet Rock* were any worse than those which occur as a matter of course in the commercial theatre. The crucial difference, however, was that the actors in *Viet Rock* were not performing the usual fiction, but a play which they had helped create through improvisational workshop. Miss Terry has described the evolution of *Viet Rock* as follows: "The playwright experiments with the actors on movement and visual images, but then he goes home and writes the play, including the words." This is a simplification: in the case of a workshop-created play it is really not possible objectively to separate the writer's contributions from those of the actors. Most of the *Viet Rock* cast considered themselves authors also. They were especially sensitive to changes of staging or dialogue, to realignment of priorities, to Miss Terry's assumption of total control over the production.

Viet Rock had opened off-Broadway to generally poor reviews, including a blast from Walter Kerr of the all-important *New York Times*. After six weeks it closed.

In the final scene of *Viet Rock*, the GIs are on leave in Saigon. They are carousing in a bar with Vietnamese girls; there is an explosion; everybody dies. From the motionless heap of actors' bodies on the floor comes the chorus of phrases from which I have already quoted the "Who needs war" passage. This merges into the coda of the play, for which Miss Terry's instructions are as follows:

> . . . the entire company says the following together and the heap should pulse like a giant beating heart.
>
> WHO WHO WHO
> WHO WHO WHO
> WHO WHO WHO
> WHO——!
>
> As the last line dies away there is silence for a count of twenty. Then one by one the actors rise. They must do so in extremely slow motion as if coming back from a long distance. They are fragile. They are angels. They are beautiful. One by one they stand. One by one they enter the audience. Each chooses an audience member and touches his hand, head, face, hair. Look and touch. Look and touch. A celebration of presence. They go among the audience until every actor has left the stage. Then as the song begins they leave the auditorium. In no way should the actors communicate superiority. They must communicate the wonder and gift of being actually alive together with the audience at that moment.

The actors come into the audience: actors-as-people, not actors-as-characters. They touch members of the audience. Can you repudiate touch? You can disbelieve what you are told, what you are shown, but can you disbelieve being touched? Being touched makes you recognize that you are alive, there and then.

One of the questions which preoccupy the theatre today: who is alive? Is the actor alive? Is the spectator alive? The traditional theatre supplants the actor's life with the character's life. Several characters interact in a series of events determined ahead of time by the playwright and, in rehearsals, by the director and the cast. Each performance of the play aims to be identical to each other performance. Change in this fictive world is not only not endorsed; it is evaded. The traditional theatre, from the Greeks to naturalism, freezes what it extrapolates from real life and repeats it in identical form night after night. Yet in life, change is an incontrovertible reality. Put a puppy on the stage and the audience forgets about the actors. Why? Because a puppy could do anything; it is mindless, shameless and unconscious of being observed. The actor, on the other hand, can do only what he is programmed to do within the matrix of his character. The audience knows that he is not alive, there and then.

Neither is the spectator alive in most forms of traditional theatre. Spectators as people are crucial to the *structure* of the theatre, receiving, appreciating, financing the enterprise. But they do not participate as alive in the event. Especially in the naturalistic play, the actors are alone on stage, behaving as if nobody at all were looking on from the auditorium, which is conceived to be a separate room. The Method claims the actor for naturalism: it trains him to become unaware of the spectator. Theatre for children, where the audience is directly addressed, wooed, cajoled, is an exception. Broadway musicals also woo the audience, if clumsily, and the pleasure of being treated as alive is one reason for which people flock to them.

The new theatre of the sixties rejects the traditional non-life of the actor and of the spectator. In this there is a strong influence from Brecht. Brecht wanted the theatre to be an instrument for social change, so he used it as a rational examination of the nature of human events. He wanted to lead the audience to question tacit assumptions about the universality and immutability of human nature. Against the claim that human nature cannot change, Brecht asserted that human nature is not fixed; things could be different if we willed them to be. His particular and peculiar dramaturgy, revolving around the difficult concept of the alienation-effect, was his attempt to make that assertion in theatrical terms. Alienation requires the actor to create his character within the narrative while at the same time standing apart from that creation in order to comment on it as a person independent of the fiction: the actor aims to come on stage as character and person at the same time. As character he advances the narrative; as person he communicates directly to the spectators whom he assumes to be alive and present. The procedure contributed to Brecht's overall goal of inducing the spectators to realize that the dramatic action—the fiction—was an exemplary tale from which to draw moral conclusions about how life should and could be lived.

The alienation-effect itself is rarely visible in the American theatre. What of Brecht has been pervasive in the new theatre of the sixties, however, is his assumption that theatre is essentially an exchange between live men on the stage and live men in the seats, and that the exchange aims to affect the way that the latter will henceforth conduct themselves. In his 1968 *Village Voice* article paying tribute to the Becks, Chaikin said:

> I believe that the ultimate value in the theatre is the confrontation of all the live bodies in the room with the mortality which they share: the visceral confrontation with the reality that one is living now and at some other time no longer living.

EXPECTING

One of Chaikin's investigations of ways to open up the sense of mortality at the theatre event is known as expecting. If the actor is to come on stage as a man, and if he is to treat the audience as alive, he must deliberately expand his sense of other people. The tendency to see others as cardboard figures, as extensions of their jobs, as less human than oneself, must be broken down; the actor must learn to see the fullness and complexity of another person. The expecting work builds toward this by developing the actor's ability to control his concept of who other people are. The work is based on elementary psychological facts: that the information which you have about a person influences your attitude toward him (he is rich, therefore worthy); that your attitude toward him influences your behavior toward him (he is worthy, therefore I will be nice); that your behavior toward him influences *his* behavior toward you (I am nice to him, therefore he is nice to me), and *also* influences his attitude (he begins to feel superior). Expecting demonstrates that you can induce a person to manifest a particular quality by expecting it of him.

In terms of behavior, one sees expecting operate in the transformation exercise. As one actor suddenly treats his partner like a dog, he expects his partner to become a dog, and given the structure of the transformation the partner rapidly does so. In the expecting work proper, however, the actors are concerned with their relationship to the audience. They decide who the audience is and then strive in their improvisation to act in such a way that the audience will participate in that identity. Some identities used in the workshop: the audience is a group of Nazis, of saints, of colossally stupid people; the audience is a collection of the people whom the actor admires most in the world; it is a group of the actor's alter ego.

Chaikin has devised several improvisational structures and exercises for expecting. One framework has several actors line up facing the rest of the group, who are the audience for the purpose of the exercise. Among themselves, the exercising actors decide on the identity of the audience, perhaps Fascist police looking for members of the underground. That is the actors' "secret information." Then the workshop leader asks the actors simple questions in a neutral tone of voice ("what is your name?"; "where do you live?"; "what is your job?"; "do you have a big wardrobe?"). The actors respond according to their secret information, trying through their tone and behavior to arouse in the audience the feelings of superiority, control, and power over others characteristic of Fascist police. This will happen if the actors can believe the secret information and let that belief inform the way they answer the questions; they should avoid playing the secret information. The exercise can be reversed, where the "audience" possesses the secret information and endows the actors in the line-up with a matching quality by means of the tone of the questioning. Another structure for the expecting exercise sets one actor to telling a story to the rest of the workshop as audience, and he shifts his expectation of them in the course of it. He does this by deciding on two pieces of secret information, concentrating on one for a while, then on the other. The goal still is to get the members of the audience to participate in the qualities which the narrator expects of them.

As an improvisation, expecting has a simple structure: several actors improvise a simple scene, such as a court case. First they run through it with one idea of the audience—saints, for example; then with another—say, political anarchists. One thing to be observed in such an improvisation is the manner in which the assumed identity of the audience

EXPANSION AND STRUGGLE / 85

influences the choices which the actors make in their improvising.

Expecting is a continuing investigation at the Open Theatre. Chaikin considers it to be potentially useful in acting material of which the idea structure and moral values cannot be assumed to be shared by the audience; if the actor can endow the audience with qualities pertinent to such material, he can reach them intellectually or ideologically.

Although the Open Theatre has not made expecting into a reliable technique, the device has been successfully used in performance. This was the coda of *Viet Rock*, where the actors touched the audience physically. In order to arouse a sense of life among the spectators, the cast deliberately needed to expect it. Their secret information was that the audience was a group of creatures which the actors had never before seen, and their task was simply to notice this life. When a member of the audience blinked an eye, that was a dramatic and wondrous action because the actor was seeing it for the first time. The heightened sense of life projected by the actors conveyed to the audience a sense of rebirth, following the death and destruction in the play's final scene. The coda accomplished what Miss Terry calls the "celebration of life."

The device was a controversial one. At Yale, for example, Brustein thought it was silly and asked the cast to jettison it. I observed that many members of the audiences there and elsewhere found it very moving. Chaikin thought it became sentimentalized with repetition, a matter merely of "making nice to each other." Miss Terry might ask, "What's wrong with that?" and so would I.

∞

SUCCESS AND FAILURE 5

Four days before *Viet Rock* opened to its killing reviews at the Martinique, van Itallie's three-play collection *America Hurrah* opened at the Pocket Theatre. This was an independent production, and the Open Theatre name did not appear on the program; however, approximately half of the cast and the two directors, as well as the author, were members of the troupe. *America Hurrah* became a hit, to the surprise of almost everyone connected with the production, due essentially to Walter Kerr's favorable review in the *New York Times* and Robert Brustein's in the *New Republic*. The unfavorable notices, such as the *Village Voice* review by Ross Wetzsteon, who admired the production but not the plays, had little effect on the thriving box office.

The three plays of *America Hurrah* are *Interview*, an expansion and reworking of *Pavane*; *TV*, a play written for the occasion; and *Motel*, which van Itallie wrote before he joined the Open Theatre and which had been first produced under the title of *America Hurrah* on a bill with *Pavane* at the Cafe La MaMa in 1965.

To my mind, *Interview* is the best of the three plays, and in Chaikin's production it was one of the finest of all the Open Theatre's presentations. The play deals with the ice age in which we live—surrounded by people, yet isolated, alienated, mechanized. The scenes state variations on this theme: a young woman, eager to find a bargain in the shopping district, gets lost in a hostile crowd of anonymous and threatening street types; a middle-aged business executive, suffering from the breakdown of his single relationship—to his tv set—consults a psychiatrist who offers him formulas; a housepainter, whose artistic frustrations represent his total alienation, turns to his confessor, as he always does, who has nothing to say, as he never has. Each thematic variation, after the job interview scene—an ensemble construction which opens the play—is set up as a solo for one of the eight actors, with the rest of the company forming an ensemble of support. In musical terms, *Interview* is an oratorio with an opening chorus, eight arias supported by the chorus and linked by short choral passages, and a closing chorale recapitulating the aria motifs.

During his solo, each actor speaks to the audience directly, narrating rather than enacting the experience of his character. Here is some of the lost woman's speech:

> ... I saw someone right in front of me and I said, could you direct me please to Fourteenth Street, I have to get to Fourteenth Street, please, to get a bargain, I explained, although I could hardly remember what it was I wanted to buy. I read about it in the paper today, I said, only they weren't listening and I said to myself, my purpose for today is to get to—and I couldn't remember, I've set myself the task of—I've got to have—it's that I can save, I remembered, I can save if I can get that bargain at—and I couldn't remember where it was so I started to look for my wallet which I seem to have mislaid in my purse, and a man—please watch where you're going, I shouted with my purse half-open, and I seemed to forget—Fourteenth Street, I remembered, and you'd think with all these numbered streets and avenues a person wouldn't get lost—you'd think a person would HELP a person, you'd think so. . . .

Chaikin directed the actors to focus intimately on the audience during the solos, as if they were speaking to themselves. The intimacy between the actors and the audience effected in this way put the characters' alienation from one another in sharp relief. Also it aroused the audience's empathy, which struck a balance with the effect of the play's sharp mockery and satire. *Interview* has a bright surface and a hard-edged contour expressive of the world it is about, yet it engages one's sentiment as well.

The play is rich in Open Theatre techniques, some indicated by van Itallie in writing the play, others evoked by Chaikin in producing it. (They are all incorporated into the play as printed since the text was finalized after the play was produced.) Some of them—machines, unnoticed action, inside-outside—I have already indicated. Another is "the phrase," a device which Chaikin had developed in workshop during the preceding season.

THE PHRASE
A phrase is a brief sound and/or movement which the actor repeats in identical form a specified number of times or for a specified period of time as the paradigm of a character. it constitutes the entire characterization; thus, although it is naturalistic in form, it is emblematic in function. Given its severe delimitation and the repetition, a phrase has a ritualistic effect and tends to depersonalize character; inevitably it suggests automatons and types, either social types or archetypes. A scene composed of phrased characterizations takes on a formal rhythm and an abstract composition. But it possesses the extra force of all aesthetic statements which follow the rule of less-is-more.

The supporting action for the lost woman's solo in the Fourteenth Street scene, from which I have quoted, is the phased action in *Interview*. While the girl talks to the audience downstage and facing front, the seven other actors are ranged in a line across the back of the stage. Each actor adopts a characterization of an urban street type expressed in a phrase and repeats it over and over as he walks down to the front of the stage and then right back upstage again, where he chooses another phrase and moves down again as another character. Thus do seven actors embody a great number and variety of passersby.

Phrases are related to Brecht's "gestus" and also to the ideograms of the classical Chinese theatre. In the latter, which Chaikin says were his inspiration for the device, the actor makes use of specific gestures to characterize particular archetypal characters. Death, for example, does a unique wave of the arm when he enters the scene: this identifies him instantly to an audience acquainted with the traditional forms. At the Open Theatre, the actor creates a phrase by an imaginative leap or by selecting it from among the elements surfacing in an improvisation on character. Indeed, the phrase is a means of preserving elements of improvisation for performance—of recording them for future use, as it were. Chaikin sets the actors to exercising with phrases from time to time as a check on the unwieldy and generalized aspects of improvisation.

∞

татв, the second play of *America Hurrah*, is more conventional than *Interview*, but it implements an ingenious idea. There are two groups of characters, and at the beginning of the play they occupy separate areas of the stage. One group are employees of a television rating service who sit facing the audience at a tv control console at the front of the stage and to the left. The other group are actors who perform the tv shows, commercials and newscasts being rated; they stand frozen at the rear of the stage and to the right; that is, as far from the raters as possible. The play is made up of scenes of real life in the viewing room played in alternation with scenes of tv action. There is a marked and ironic contrast in the quality of life, however: where the real life is flat, insipid, tedious, the tv life is dynamic, lively, full of emotional display. As the play progresses, the tv action preempts more and more of the stage, gradually taking over the viewing room itself. By the end of the play, the tv segments are being performed in the laps of the raters, who show no awareness of the invasion. The final scene is a double one: the tv people play out a situation comedy which neatly parallels what is going on among the raters at the same time. In the last hideous moment everyone laughs the brutish laughter of canned television shows; the real people have been subsumed by the fake.

Jacques Levy, who was to start an Open Theatre workshop that season, directed *TV*. His production was skillful but too funny for the good of the play; that is, the television parody was so clever and one enjoyed it so much that the dullards in the rating room came to seem like annoying interlopers, rather than the subjects of the play's concern.

The third play of *America Hurrah, Motel,* is a virtuoso ten-minute exposure of the violent, destructive revel of contemporary America life. Van Itallie says that he was inspired to write it by Artaud's *The Theatre and its Double.* There are three characters, all of them life-sized dolls with actors inside. The motel-keeper is the archetypal domestic: homey, bland, loquacious, absorbed in her possessions. A disembodied recording of her voice enumerating the contents and merits of her rooms, one of which is the setting of the action, constitutes the verbal score of the play. Two travelers arrive, move in, and set about defacing and destroying everything in the room, ignoring the motel-keeper and her monologue. Nor does she notice them, but drones steadily on. The tension between the two situations builds up. Eventually, as the action approaches a blinding, deafening, stunning pitch, with sirens screaming and lights flashing, the travelers destroy the motel-keeper as one more object in the defeated room and race from the scene. Then, abruptly, there is a black-out and silence. As directed by Levy, *Motel* was a knock-out, going a long way, I think, toward capturing for *America Hurrah* the admiration which it enjoyed for the year or more of its off-Broadway run.

As soon as *America Hurrah* opened, the workshops reconvened. The first new project was political. During the summer and fall of 1966, many New York artists banded together as the "Angry Artists Against the War in Vietnam." Painters, poets, dancers, sculptors, mixed media artists, musicians and theatre artists were doing exhibitions, readings, and playlets on street corners and in churches. The Open Theatre became part of the loose organization. *Viet Rock* had focused the group's animus against the war, and Chaikin's and Feldman's dissatisfaction with the tone of the work had intensified the matter. The troupe threw itself into preparations and created a program which had the occasional tone and improvisatory spirit of the 1965 programs. It was put on twice at the end of January 1967.

Feldman directed two scenes. The first, known as "State of the Union," had been prepared for *Viet Rock,* but Miss Terry had objected to it and it had not been included. The corpse of a dead soldier was brought in on a stretcher, and mourners arrived to pay respects to the widow. As they sat in reverent attitudes before the body, President Johnson's voice was heard expounding on domestic affairs—social security payments, Medicare, crime in the streets—from his 1967 State of the Union speech. One by one the mourners, including the widow, rose, went over to the corpse, and broke off pieces of the body to devour. As this mimed feast continued, the recording of Johnson's voice got stuck in a groove, and he drawled over and over again, "This nation must make an all-out effort to combat crime." The scene evolved imperceptibly from the naïveté of its premise to the bitterest irony, and in the juxtaposition of elements effected a peculiar horror.

Feldman's other scene was even more explicit. Called "Building the Soldiers," it was based on the body-molding exercise. Two actors molded two others into soldiers and taught them how to fight. Additional actors repeated set phrases from the terminology of the war—"demilitarized zone," "search and destroy"—in the objective style of newscasters. A voice over a loudspeaker interrupted the action from time to time with a brief statement by Bertrand Russell against the war, but the creation of the soldiers went forward unaffected. When the soldiers existed, the instructors transformed into a television camera team and recorded their attack on each other. During this section, the newscasters repeated the phrase "human shield incident," a term which the *New York Times* had used in reference to an action in Vietnam. After the soldiers killed each other, the members of the camera team shook hands as if congratulating each other on their excellent footage.

The other noteworthy event of the Angry Arts program, besides the annual presentation of *The Clown Play*, was an innovation on the chord. After doing the ritual in a circle, the actors turned to the audience, left the playing area, and went up the aisles of the theatre while keeping the resonance going. The idea was to embrace the audience with the warm, ensemble dynamic. It was a controversial attempt:

Chaikin and Feldman thought that communion and affirmation pervaded the room; Michael Smith thought that nothing happened.

In his workshop, which met once a week, Chaikin devoted a good deal of time to philosophizing. His priority was to reestablish some cohesion in the troupe—decimated by the strife of the late spring and summer, by the energy loss of doing two commercial productions, by the division into two casts, one coping with success, the other with failure. During long breaks in the exercising and improvisation he talked to the company, sharing things from Brecht, from Artaud, from Peter Brook, things he had heard, things he had read, particularly from the existential philosophers. He amplified these "pebbles," as he called them, with his own thoughts, worries, fears, and concerns. He told anecdotes illustrating insights which he had, confusions which he could not resolve, human problems on the social and personal level which perturbed and upset him. He wanted to open the actors' minds and hearts to the continuing moral dilemma of an existence which seemed to him increasingly alien.

> We have to shake off the sophistication of our time, by which we close ourselves up, and to become vulnerable again. We realize that life hasn't been too generous with us, and we've retreated. We've closed off a great deal of our total human response. But as actors we must open up again, become naive again, innocent, and cultivate our deeper climates—our dread, for example. Only then will we be able to find new ways to express the attitudes which we hold in common with the outside world, and ways to express the attitudes which we hold as uniquely our own.

Chaikin urged the actors to go into the "temples and prisons" of the larger community for insight and inspiration: to night court, mental hospitals, meetings of Alcoholics Anonymous, religious services—places and events which would put them in contact with deeper realities than the experience of commercial play production, in which they were engaged.

Chaikin was influenced here by his association with Julius Orlovsky, a catatonic schizophrenic according to the hospital from which he had just been released, about whom Robert Frank was making a movie. Chaikin was playing Orlovsky for the project, and he was improvising much of the verbal text himself. He and Orlovsky spent time together and became friends. Chaikin felt that he was learning a great deal from Orlovsky, of whose knowledge of human suffering he grew more and more awed. Yet as specifically as he was interested in Orlovsky, Chaikin saw him as a representative. "Among the people in difficulty whom I know," he told me, "I see Julius as the common denominator of all our bewilderment. As much as one feels for him, or any person in trouble one knows, he's only one of several. When you take Julius to the doctor, and there are twenty people in the waiting room, eighteen of them are worse off than he is." (Frank's movie *Me and My Brother* was released in 1969.)

The Open Theatre company received Chaikin's promptings cautiously. His personal eloquence and the depth of his concern made his ideas relevant at the moment of exchange, but there seemed to be little cumulative effect. Because of the off-Broadway productions several members of the troupe saw themselves in a new light: as performers devoting energies to pleasing people and earning praise. A few of them had agents who were receiving and transmitting offers. Such outside distractions kept the rifts within the troupe from healing. Chaikin had closed his workshop against newcomers; yet that seemed to make for an atmosphere in which some disagreements only heated up.

Given the prevailing atmosphere, it was not surprising that these workshops emphasized physical techniques rather than ensemble improvisation. The Open Theatre had not been a place of elementary training. Voice, speech, body movement, and acting skills were matters left to the members to pursue outside. But Chaikin's experience during the previous summer made him want to alter this. He had spent several weeks in London as a consultant to Peter Brook's *US* workshop at the Royal Shakespeare Theatre, where he worked with a group of traditionally trained English actors. He also encountered Jerzy Grotowski, the director of the Polish Lab Theatre and another of Brook's consultants, and observed the presentation of his tightly organized, rigorously disciplined exercises. He had returned home determined that the Open Theatre should work ten times harder than in the past.

Chaikin introduced the Open Theatre to "the Cat" and the associated Grotowski exercises. Coincidentally, two members of the workshop had also learned the Grotowski techniques during the previous summer: Seth Allen and Jacque Lynn Colton had studied with Eugenio Barba, one of Grotowski's former disciples, at his theatre in Denmark, where they were touring with the La MaMa troupe. What follows here is the sequence as corrected by Grotowski when he visited the workshop the following year.

THE CAT
(1) Lie on your stomach and clear your mind. Relax and be aware of the various parts of your body touching the floor.

(2) Wake your body up, "like a cat getting ready to spring." Stretch your arms out in all directions. Placing the palms of your hands flat on the floor next to your shoulders, lift your head slowly and turn it in various directions, stretching your neck. Raise your chest slowly off the floor, shifting your weight gradually to your hands. At the point where your chest is completely off the floor, lock your elbows and knees, tuck your toes under, and raise your body as high as it will go, stretching up from your hands and feet in an arch of which your buttocks are the apex. (3) Flex that arch several times by dropping your buttocks and snapping your head up, then immediately raising your buttocks and dropping your head. (4) Walk your feet up toward your hands and back again; walk your hands back toward your feet and forward again. (5) In the push-up position, but with your head and shoulders lowered slightly, imagine that a small ball is rolling slowly down your spinal column, vertebra by vertebra, from the small of your back to your head. When the ball gets to your neck, realign your body so that it will roll slowly back where it came from. Repeat several times. (6) Swivel your body at at your hips, bending the knees and swooping down toward the floor. (7) Again in the push-up position, turn your body so that you face to the side. Bring the knee of your upper leg toward your ear and stretch your head toward it over your shoulder. At the same time, push your foot out and away, in an attempt to extend the leg. This is like a fight between your upper and lower leg, with the latter eventually winning. Repeat with the other leg. (8) Duck one shoulder under and roll over onto your back.

THE BIG TOWER

Lying on your back, bend your arms and legs, putting the palms and soles flat on the floor. Raise your stomach in an arch, straightening your arms. Relax back onto the floor.

THE CANDLE

Lying on your back, raise your legs and buttocks off the floor, supporting your back with your hands. Get as much of your back as possible off the floor by pushing your rib cage toward your chin and higher and higher. Point your toes at the ceiling. Now drop one leg and let the other follow to the floor behind your head. Flex your feet. Separate your feet about eight inches. Point your toes and, still pushing your rib cage, drop your knees to the floor next to your ears. Now straighten your legs again. Raise your right leg in the air. Bend both knees and let the left leg come up a little. Keep pushing your rib cage and extend your right leg down toward the floor. When your right foot hits the floor you are in a split, with your left leg still over your head. Now rock: right leg up and left leg down; then left leg up and right leg down. Reverse legs.

THE SMALL TOWER

Kneel on the floor, your knees and feet apart. Let your hands and arms hang down relaxed at your sides. Thrust your pelvis forward and lean back slowly, arching your back until your head touches the floor. Relax your body so that your head, shoulders and buttocks make contact with the floor. Now make a sharp impulse from the middle of your body to pull yourself up; spring forward, letting your head and shoulders hang back so that you are arching again. Let yourself fall forward and roll in the arched position.

THE HEAD STAND

Get on your hands and knees. Touch the top of your head to the floor and put your hands palms down next to your knees. Lift your hips into the air and lock your knees. Now walk up as far as possible, straightening your spine. Your points of balance are your head and your hands. Shift your weight off your toes onto that triangle of support. Point your feet at the ceiling. (If necessary, do an intermediate step: rest your knees on your elbows before raising your feet into the air.) Return to kneeling position.

THE SHOULDER STAND
Lie prone with one cheek on the floor. Bring your hand on the side you are facing to shoulder level and place it palm down on the floor; point your elbow up. Let your other arm rest on the floor alongside your body. Keeping your knees locked, raise your hips off the floor. Raise them as high as they will go by walking toward your shoulders and around toward the raised arm. Find your balance: the points of balance are your cheek, the hand which you are facing, and the shoulder of your other arm. Shift your weight onto that triangle of support. Raise your feet and legs into the air. Return to prone position.

SLOW-MOTION WALK
Get up. Move around the work area in slow motion. Try to stay on tiptoe. From time to time, sink to the floor, turn somersaults, etc., but all in coordinated slow motion.

TENSE-UP
Standing still, strain every part of your body, achieving the maximum possible tension. Take the time to tense all your muscles. Then abruptly let all the tension go, relaxing everything. You will fall down (and not get hurt, since your body is relaxed). Get up and jump slightly in the air, trying to slap your knees against your chest several times.

These exercises are intended to be done as a sequence without rests. Keeping the sequence is important since one of the goals is that the physical tasks become automatic. Resting between exercises should be avoided in order to develop oneself physically (Grotowski talks about "working past one's fatigue"), and in order to minimize reflection, fear, self-consciousness, awareness of others. The point is to be alone with oneself, not to worry about what one's work looks like or what the work of others looks like. It is understood that the exercises are hard to do. But failure—losing balance, or falling—should be incorporated into the rhythm of the total sequence. It helps to sing a song in one's head and keep all the movements, even the accidents, in rhythm with the song. If an accident should break the rhythm, one can make up one's own melody for that part, and then return to the song. The important thing is to keep the process going from first to last exercise.

∞

The difficulty of these exercises brought the Open Theatre company to a higher level of physical strength and control. It would remain for Grotowski himself to impart the intention and spirit of his "psycho-physical" work to the troupe during his visits to the workshop the following fall, but during the 1966–67 workshop the company laid a foundation of technical expertise.

The Grotowski exercises figured prominently in a workshop which Lee Worley started for newcomers to the Open Theatre. But Miss Worley was also concerned with the ensemble techniques slighted by Chaikin's workshop; indeed, she undertook her workshop in order to recapture the ensemble spirit lacking in Chaikin's. She spent a great deal of time on worlds, the chord, trusting exercises, inside-outside, the conductor. After Chaikin, Miss Worley is the member of the troupe most enticed by the vision of an ensemble theatre existing outside the commercial mainstream. An excellent teacher, she is also a diligent student of the subtle distinction between acting and performing.

LIFE MASKS

One of Miss Worley's exercises is life masks, where the actors attempt to transform their faces from instruments of concealment into instruments of communication. Standing in a circle, they contort and limber their face muscles and then relax into neutral or "sleep" masks. Each actor thinks of a line which conveys a sharp attitude or has a strong emotional meaning to him, such as "the world is awful" or "the sunshine is marvelous." To a slow count of five, provided by the workshop leader, the actor "feeds" the line to his face—that is, he searches for the proper facial expression of the attitude or emotion behind the line. At five, he shows his life mask to those near him; then he releases it to another slow count of five.

The essentials are, first, that the actor does not arbitrarily pick a facial mask which fits his line, but by mobilizing his facial muscles seeks a mask which expresses the line, and secondly, that he keeps feeding the line to his mask after it is found, so that it does not become a lifeless contortion.

The actor can add sound to his mask or, in a variant of the exercise, he can do the sound to another actor's mask. In the latter case, the second actor should choose the line to feed to his sound by freely associating from the first actor's mask, rather than by adopting the line which he supposes the first actor to be using.

∞

FACE CONVERSATION

Face conversation was developed out of the life masks exercise in 1968.

After relaxing the facial muscles, the actors pair off and decide on a topic to discuss. Using only the face, including the mouth but without speech, they then have a discussion. As in many Open Theatre procedures, the trick is to follow along and allow something to happen without choosing. As an improvisation Chaikin explains face conversation as follows:

> I've often thought that any two people have something of their own to express to each other which they share with no other people—some special something which belongs to them, or happens only between them. This even applies to people who pass on the street. That thing probably couldn't be found in speech; spoken things are too easy to classify; it would no longer seem special. But it can probably be found, and expressed, in a kind of dialogue with the face.

Miss Worley extends the improvisation by having the actors add their shoulders to the conversation, then their arms, torsos, legs, and finally, their voices (in sounds rather than speech). After using their full resources for a time, the actors subtract their voices, but make sounds with their bodies—slapping, stomping, snapping, etc.

∞

Jacques Levy's workshop of 1966–67 was an attempt to create a play by means of a full-scale collaboration among actors, writers, directors and composers—what Brook had done in creating *US*. Levy's intention was to build a play on the theme of assassination, focusing on the killing of President Kennedy, but the project broke down in the difficulty which the three writers (Miss Fornes, Miss Thie, and van Itallie) experienced in collaborating. And Levy left the Open

Theatre the following summer to pursue his career as a stage director.

Levy's influence on the Open Theatre was considerable. He worked much more objectively with the actors than Chaikin does, yet with great sensitivity to their problems. He was also a valuable intellectual stimulus, capable of articulating the Open Theatre's ideas and values and helping define them in the process. He was also ambitious for the Open Theatre, and by his efforts lines of communication were opened between the troupe and the foundations.

Characteristically, Chaikin did not block Levy's incentive although he was not interested in its goal. He saw the opportunities which Levy sought as so many bribes to be resisted. He felt that the troupe still suffered from the abrasive relationships of its previous and current outside involvements. Relationships backstage at *America Hurrah,* which ran through the entire season, were in fact growing steadily worse. Even van Itallie, who most valued the off-Broadway production, saw that the energy which had once gone into making the plays better and better was now being usurped by the dissension among the cast.

In the spring, Chaikin agreed to cooperate with a production of *America Hurrah* at the Royal Court Theatre in London. He saw this as the chance to investigate the possibilities of relocating the troupe to Europe, setting up in a city there, or becoming a peripatetic troupe like the Living Theatre. In his pessimism, moreover, voluntary exile from the lures of life in America came readily to his mind.

The final session of Chaikin's 1966–67 workshop occurred in May as the first session at new quarters. St. Peter's Lutheran

Church had invited the troupe to use its empty facilities free of charge. The actors were enthusiastic about the ample work space, and they did the most gregarious and rambunctious warm-up of any session I have seen. But Chaikin was glum. He talked to the company about the arrogance of that year's workshop atmosphere, about the clashes of temperament which had resulted from the closed-door policy, and about the false starts, the detours, the lack of a through-line in the work. There had been great inertia, and tensions of the damaging rather than the fruitful sort. All in all Chaikin saw the year as the Open Theatre's worst.

He volunteered that part of the trouble had been his own ambivalence about the subject matter which he thought the troupe should pursue. His principal purpose still was the transcendental use of the stage: "to people the stage with monsters and saints that exist in the mind," as he had put it in a radio interview (WBAI-FM, April 22, 1967). Yet political events in America alarmed him, and he considered it frivolous to ignore the war, the civil rights struggle, the student rebellion. He yearned to concentrate on works like *The Dybbuk*, *Woyzeck*, and *Nightwood* (the Djuna Barnes novel, which he wanted to dramatize), but he felt that the troupe must first put together an adequate statement of political protest, and he requested the several writers then associated with the troupe to send him political material during the summer.

This tension between "the inner" and "the outer" had long been a fact of life in Chaikin's work, as in that of many of his colleague innovators of the new theatre: the Becks, Brook, Grotowski, Schechner. The outer, as we have seen, derives from Brecht, from both his theoretical writing and his plays. The inner comes from Artaud's vision of a transcendental, ceremonial, sacrificial theatre which would reveal man's life as a kind of psychic seizure. From its inception, the Open Theatre had pursued now the line of the inner, now of the outer, shifting back and forth from the abstract section of "The Odets Kitchen" to the naturalistic section, from "The Illusion Scene" to the Doris plays, from *Motel* to *Viet Rock*. In the winter and spring of 1967, the claims of the two modes had brought Chaikin's workshop to a grinding halt artistically. And it was on this note that he closed down his workshop at the end of the season.

In the fall of 1967, however, Chaikin embarked on a course of work which led to a recognizable and interesting synthesis of the inner-outer duality and, in consequence, to the production of the Open Theatre's first mature work of art. This was *The Serpent,* a collaboration between Chaikin's workshop and van Itallie as writer-architect. Of this work, while it was still in progress and the end not yet in sight, Chaikin would say: "The inner and the outer—there's the impossible study."

"THE IMPOSSIBLE STUDY" 6

The Open Theatre organized for 1967–68 in a rented loft on Bleecker Street, St. Peter's Church having thrown the group out after a rowdy sound-and-movement during the summer. Almost 100 people came to the first session; most of them were actors who had heard that the Open Theatre was opening up to new blood. For them Rhea Gaisner announced an eight-week series of workshops on basic techniques, at the end of which some people would be invited into other workshops and the rest would be expected to leave. For old members there were several projects. Feldman announced his intention to build an anti-war play; Miss Terry wanted to pursue matters left undone after the *Viet Rock* workshop; Miss Worley would continue her workshop on an intermediate level. All of these were to meet once a week. For his part, Chaikin announced a workshop to meet four days a week, four hours a day; he said he wanted to work on the Bible.

During the summer Chaikin had decided to do his new workshop with new actors. He was disgusted with the old company. The brush-up rehearsals with the original *America Hurrah* cast in preparation for London confirmed his disappointment with the 1966–67 workshop. The old company might have had the best abilities in the Open Theatre, but their attitudes seemed to Chaikin to disqualify them for serious new work. Chaikin wanted actors who would be "available" to the workshop inquiry. In part this meant relative egolessness: an actor's willingness to be used in workshop to serve the investigation. In rehearsal for a public production, an actor has had his role assigned, has adjusted to its dimension, and knows how he fits into the total project. But in Chaikin's workshop, where an actor functions as a tool in research, his position is not clear. And he begins to suffer from boredom, the sensation of being *de trop,* lack of praise or even comment on something he has done, seeing his work discarded. Many actors cannot take this; others cannot take it gracefully. Another aspect of an actor's "availability" is his willingness to enter areas where he feels uncertain. Most actors know what kind of behavior gets them results; they have their tried and true expressive means. But in Chaikin's workshop, where the *usual* is not the subject of inquiry, the actor must be willing to reverse or ignore his safe procedures, and this can be very difficult.

Chaikin likes to work with young or new actors who haven't yet built up their personal system of safe procedures. They are less habit-ridden, more willing to take risks, more persistent, more flexible and pliant both physically and spiritually. He can work with less strife, which is important to *his* sense of safety. Young actors require Chaikin to interpose less facade; he can expose himself more. Related to this is his preference for actors who stay clear of the commercial theatre.

> Making it in the theatre is in one way or another irresistible to everyone. To me too. But it's like the emperor's new clothes: it's something which you believe is valuable because everybody makes so much noise about it, but it really isn't valuable. For it doesn't make anybody more satisfied, nor does it elevate anybody. In order to make it, you have to groom yourself—you have to have an inoffensive personality; you have to modify yourself in many minor ways—but the ways become so many that the matter isn't minor anymore. Everybody has to do this anyway in life, but I really think that one should do the absolute minimum. The more you do—the more you try to get to the big ladder—the more you have to relinquish a certain element which our work requires. For example, when you go to parties which are profitable, you go, and you smile, and you make nice to people, and soon

you don't know yourself in a sense. You lose a connection to your real responses.

Chaikin, then, resolved to control the constituency of his workshop that year, something which he had not directly done before. He invited about fifteen actors from Miss Worley's newcomers of the previous year to be the nucleus. He supplemented them with a few actors from the new off-Broadway cast of *America Hurrah,* and a very few of the older members. He asked them for a substantial commitment to the work: to attend all four sessions a week and to take no outside jobs requiring an absence of more than two weeks during the year. He had never asked so much of actors before, and the fact that he obtained it visibly energized him. (The commitment also had the political function of keeping unwanted actors from demanding to participate.) For their part, the actors saw themselves as an elect, and this released a great deal of energy. The year started off with a surge.

Chaikin engaged teachers to train his actors, using money from a $5,000 grant which the National Endowment on the Arts had given the troupe the previous spring. Kristin Linkletter taught voice and speech; Joseph Schlichter, dance and body movement; Peter Kass, acting; Swami Satchidananda, yoga; and Richard Peaslee, singing. This extended the Open Theatre's Grotowskian emphasis on physical abilities; it made 1967-68 the year in which the troupe caught up with itself technically, a corrective to the "pure research" of previous workshops.

The company's work in dance and body movement was liberating. Schlichter is a psychotherapist who uses a movement emphasis, as well as being a dancer and choreographer. His exercises aim at establishing rapport between people on a non-verbal level.

TRAVELING, TURNING, FALLING

An actor selects a partner whom he thinks moves quite unlike himself. The partner executes an action incorporating something traveling, something turning, and something falling. Then the first actor imitates the action, copying as exactly as he can. After several tries, he allows himself to move in a way natural to him but retaining something from the imitated action. The aim is to incorporate into one's own manner of moving some alien movements which one has adopted from another. This exercise is driven by the ensemble mechanism characteristic of Chaikin's exercises.

∞

SHAKING OUT

Choose a partner and have him lie on his back on the floor and close his eyes. Tell him to relax and to let you do all the work. Gently manipulate each part of his body and try to give him the sense that you are taking care of him. (1) Start with his face, working from a position above his head. Massage his forehead, eyelids, temples, nose, chin, neck. Lift his head a few inches off the floor and swivel it to loosen the neck muscles. If he does not relax and let you support him, tell him to do so. (2) Move to his side. Take each hand and rotate it at the wrist. Then his arms, rotating, pulling, and stretching. (3) Then his feet and legs. (4) Raise his knees and push them toward his chin as far as they will go, bringing his buttocks off the floor. (5) Place his legs out straight again. Working from the side, lift the near knee and tuck the foot under the other knee. Push the raised knee away from you toward the floor, while holding down the near shoulder with your other hand. Repeat from the other side. (6) Lay his legs out straight again and straddle them. Bend over and wrap your arms around his legs over the knees, holding on to your own upperarms. Squat down just over his feet. This will pull his body toward you and lift his buttocks and back off the floor. Find your balance in this position and shake his body from side to side. (7) Roll him over on his side with his arms stretched over his head. Use the edge of your hand like a saw to press deep into the upturned side of his waist. Tell him to stretch his full length as this is happening. Do the same on the other side. (8) Roll him onto his stomach. Place his hands behind his head, his face resting on his chin. Then, standing over him, bend over, take hold of his elbows, and pull them up off the floor, bringing his upper body up too. This stretches open the chest. (9) Roll him back on his back, take both of his hands in yours, and pull him slowly to a sitting position, so that his neck and middle back will sag and stretch. Then, bracing your foot against his feet, pull him to a standing position.

∞

Chaikin commented on the Schlichter procedures like the shaking out that they enable the actor to rediscover a degree of the infant's polymorphous perversity. By giving pleasure to every part of the body *except* the genitals, they undo the genital limitation into which we grow up. It is also significant that the actors pair off to do the exercises. This helps build emotional bridges through touching. Van Itallie observes that touching in the theatre lessens the habitual tension between two actors. Like everyone else in a civilized society, actors instinctively resist touching and being touched. The shaking out is valuable because it subsumes touching to another task, making it easier for the actors to do. Chaikin has devised a few exercises which get actors to touch each other.

SLOW-MOTION WRESTLING

Here the actors pair off and wrestle in slow motion. The goal is not to win, but to achieve a balance between aggression and cooperation. As the actor exerts force against his partner, he also helps him yield to the force. For example, while he is pushing his partner to the floor, he must also hold him and ease him down. The slow motion is the key to this; in order to maintain it, the partners must aid each other even as they strive against each other.

∞

BREATHING BODIES

After some limbering exercises, actors lie on the floor, relaxing and breathing deeply. Imagining that their entire bodies are lungs, they find movements to express the regular filling and emptying of that organ—tensing and relaxing, rising and falling, sitting up and lying back, rolling over and then back, undulating the limbs. Without breaking stride, the actors take partners and continue in couples, adjusting their rhythms to a common one and always touching each other with some part of their bodies. Letting the impulses carry them by degrees to a standing position, the couples continue to "breathe"—bending at the waist, the knees, the neck; turning, twisting, flailing. After a time they change partners, adapt to each other and slowly sink back to the floor, eventually separating and stopping. Besides building bridges through touching, this exercise makes the actor cognizant of breathing, which Chaikin calls "the awareness of being."

∞

PULSING BODIES

As breathing bodies has the actor imagine that his entire body is a lung, pulsing bodies has him conceive of his body as a heart. Sitting on the floor, the actor sets up a pulse with his body—tensing and relaxing in a regular series of beats like tiny explosions. Chaikin frequently asks the actors to think about the pulses as alternations between life and death. The actors choose partners as in breathing bodies.

In both of these exercises, the actors should try to avoid censoring where they touch each other. Particularly in the passages which occur on the floor, the participants will find themselves making socially awkward contact: the face of one at the crotch of another, the buttocks of one on the other's chest, and so on. The fact that the exercises set the actors to rhythms of rising and falling only increases the sense of impropriety—if the actors let it. But these chance happenings can further one of the goals, which is to loosen constraints.

∞

Jerzy Grotowski's visits to the workshop in November reinforced the Open Theatre's commitment to the exacting discipline of his physical techniques. Grotowski observed the troupe exercise some of his techniques and some of Chaikin's. Ryszard Cieslak, a principal actor in Grotowski's company, demonstrated the techniques. And Grotowski talked. He made it clear that his physical exercises are not an end in themselves, but a means for the actor to relate his actions to his deep inner impulses. The actor should execute the movements in strict spiritual privacy and in accord with what he is experiencing emotionally or physically at the time. Thus the physical action exteriorizes his intimate, personal self. Grotowski calls this "working with associations." However, the actor does not commit the action alone, strictly speaking. He imagines the presence of a person with whom he feels maximally secure, someone in whose eyes he can do no wrong. This can be a real person, or someone whom he invents. The actor commits his psycho-physical act for this "partner in security."

Grotowski's system, the most elaborate and carefully codified acting and performance method since Stanislavski, seems to be an extension of Stanislavski's principles as amended by the theories of Artaud. The link between psychic impulse and physical behavior is Stanislavskian; the Grotowskian actor works on himself rather than off those around him. The vocabulary of non-naturalistic forms and the psychic, rather than psychological, level to which the forms relate, however, are Artaudian. Grotowski intends the actor to commit a total act, one for which he mobilizes his entire outer being (body and voice) in order to exteriorize his deepest inner being (psyche).

The encounters with Grotowski and Cieslak made the Open Theatre actors more serious. The self-conscious exhibitionism of the exercising declined; slightly but significantly the emphasis shifted away from results toward investigation and process. Thus Grotowski's visits underscored the spirit of inquiry so crucial to Chaikin's substantive workshop investigation. In fact, the actors reached the peak of their investment in that work at about this time. By December, the euphoria would decline as reality appeared at the workshop door and was admitted.

Chaikin's intention at the time of starting the Bible workshop in October had been to speculate on the events of the life of Jesus between the ages of fifteen and thirty—the period for which there is no record. He wanted to see how the rebel, the social anarchist, the moralist, and the mystic came to be. The troupe began discussing and improvising from the Book of Genesis in order to acclimate themselves to the biblical frame of reference. They asked themselves questions about life in the Garden of Eden, and improvised a zoo of imaginary animals around Adam. What was Adam's relation to these creatures and to God? What did he do when he awoke and found Eve; was he afraid, indifferent, joyful? Did he treat her as he did the animals, or was she special to him; if special, in what way? How did the serpent interest Eve in the apple? Was their encounter sexual, and if so to what degree? In what way did Eve change at the moment of biting the apple? How and why did she induce Adam to eat it?

A certain amount of discussion occurred, but the main tack, as usual, was to visualize the inquiry through improvisation. Some matters were textual. For example, the Bible says that God cursed his creatures through their own tongues, and the workshop had to find a way to make that happen theatrically. Other matters had to be considered personally. What was Adam's shame over his nakedness after eating the apple, for example, the answer to which was sought, with Schlichter's help, by the troupe's working for a time in the nude. Chaikin has referred to this work as "projecting ourselves into images and questions" associated to the events and themes of the story of Adam. The key word is "ourselves." The actors were investigating the power which the creation and damnation myth of our culture exercised in their personal lives whether they believed in it or not. They were not concerned to disprove the myth, nor to attack it, but to discover their relationship to it and to its power. Chaikin elaborates:

> There is that theatre which concerns itself with what we already know and that theatre which explores what we don't clearly know. The choice which an acting company and the actors within it make is whether they will follow the interpretations of human action which the times and society give, or follow a kind of inner speculation.

By conducting the inquiry in action, the actors were creating images (Brook's "theatre machines") in which they were sacrificially present in the Artaudian sense. Adam finding his likeness duplicated, in Eve, for the first time, then discovering the difference between them; the serpent composed of five actors, appealing to Eve on different levels of discourse; Cain killing Abel empirically for lack of a precedent; the men, as the generations of Adam, getting the women with children, then, barely changing position, being born. These were beautifully, startlingly expressive images in which, given the mode of their creation, the actors were intensely invested. Chaikin and the actors worked intimately and privately, and experienced a sense of great accomplishment.

In talking about the work, Chaikin was rhapsodic. He felt it was infused with a wholly new spirit: the actors were experimenting bravely, pushing into personally difficult areas, taking risks, exposing themselves. Chaikin seemed to have won his gamble on the new company.

The Becks had convinced Chaikin during the previous summer that he ought to take responsibility for the employment of the troupe, and he embraced the opportunity to perform in Europe. Several offers had been received, the actors were sounded out, and the plan was made to tour during the following summer. Thus the troupe began to think in terms of making a performance piece out of the Genesis work. (The idea of a piece on the life of Jesus had already been scuttled.) Chaikin, proud of the troupe's discoveries, considered the work to be about 50 per cent of an eventual piece. He began to confer with van Itallie, Miss Terry, and a newcomer, Patricia Cooper, about structuring the piece and making a text. Richard Peaslee and Stanley Walden began working on a sound score. Authorities in fields related to the work—Joseph Campbell, Susan Sontag, Paul Goodman—came to look at it and comment. The workshop became a major collaboration.

Eventually van Itallie took over the writing. His task vis-à-vis the workshop was to satisfy two demands advanced by Chaikin. First, that the additional material should in some way come out of the Biblical scenes already prepared. That meant that van Itallie's material must be concerned with exile, alienation, and man's aloneness—the principal themes of the workshop's version of the story of Adam. Secondly that the workshop dynamic of exploration and discovery should somehow be built into the eventual piece. That is, something had to be left open for the actors to investigate in *performance*. "I dream of a theatre where certain things change nightly," Chaikin had entered in a notebook several years before. Because the Bible workshop had been so nourishing and exciting to him and the actors, he wanted its process to inhere in performance.

As sensitive as van Itallie was to the demands of writing for a workshop—he more than anyone else had worked successfully in this mode—he maintained an independent vision of what the eventual Bible play would be. He came to the project as an outsider; he had not been part of the workshop during the three key months of the early improvisation. He was impressed with the work, but he had not been part of its creation, which meant that his attitude toward it differed from the actors'. Their discoveries, so precious to them, were to him a substance to be manipulated. Chaikin, of course, had to cooperate with van Itallie's attitude, for it was inevitable and justifiable despite the consequences for the actors' egos.

Chaikin's own attitude toward his new actors shifted, in fact, soon after he began to regard the Bible material as performable. Suddenly they didn't look so choice. The defect of their strength became visible; namely, that actors of extreme sensitivity where the targets are private are not volatile performers where the targets are to be shared with the public. The matter came into the open in January 1968 when it was decided to undertake benefit performances of improvisational material in order to raise money for the European tour. It devolved upon Chaikin to put together the program, although Feldman, Miss Worley, and Miss Gaisner were to prepare some scenes. The stock of the older members of the troupe shot up; indeed, a few actors who had felt distinctly unwelcome in the Bible workshop found themselves sought after. The élan of the new company fell precipitously. An open workshop, at which the new company would have been competent, would not suffice for the benefit program. The stakes were too high: a good deal of money was needed, and, in addition, the troupe was aware, perhaps for the first time, that the Open Theatre had a reputation to uphold.

There were three benefit performances: at the Pocket Theatre, the Village Gate, a night club, and St. Clement's Church. The program varied only slightly from performance to performance.

One high point was James Barbosa's brilliant interpretation of Mr. Smith in *The Clown Play*. Dazed, wide-eyed, absorbed in his pitiful needs and in the perverse satisfaction which his companions provided, Barbosa defined and integrated the character like an artifact. One was aware of the actor working behind the character, which made the portrayal extremely moving.

On the lighter side, the company did a satirical set improvisation called "Sunday Morning." The climax was an unnoticed action sequence with all the stops pulled out: during a coffee-klatsch which followed a church service, the congregation discussed what gift to give the women who had addressed the envelopes. The discussion was serious and sober; the unnoticed actions were the most elaborate and excessive sexual gropes.

The troupe did some ensemble improvisations—nervously dominated by the older members—and also performed "State of the Union" from the Angry Arts program.

The climax of the performances was a highly successful attempt to break down the invisible wall between performers and spectators, an event which was no less wonderful to experience for its being based on conventional song and dance. Some musicians played the folk song "Wild Mountain Thyme," an actress started to sing, others joined in, they began to dance. Over and over they sang the beautiful chorus of the song, louder and louder, more and more taken up by the music, but focusing directly on the audience. Other members of the troupe appeared with bunches of mimosa and began passing it out to the audience; some threw it from the stage. The spectators were moved to sway, to tap their feet, to clap in time. A warmth suffused the theatre. One began to feel closer to one's companions, to the actors, to the other spectators. It was the spirit of the new theatre—the gesture of solidarity between performers and spectators, the sense of being alive there and then. The company descended into the aisle, still singing, giving it to us, and went up to the back of the theatre, where we found them as we left. At the second benefit, the company and spectators could dance in the open spaces between the tables of the Village Gate. At one point, these areas being crowded, the company burst back up to the stage, where they stopped dancing, faced the audience and sang the chorus over and over very full and loud. By this simple and straightforward means, the event of the benefit performance was lifted from the ordinary and transformed.

For all that these evenings were pick-up programs and some of the pieces uninteresting, they had a great sense of life. One expects more than exhilaration of the Open Theatre, of course, but from other theatres one often gets less. Although Harold Clurman voiced the reservations common to intellectuals discussing group blow-outs, he described the effect of the program as "tonic" and advised his readers in the *Nation* to "look out for the Open Theatre!"

The high spirits of the benefit programs, however, did not carry over to the Bible workshop. The troupe's morale steadily declined, hitting bottom in early May just before the premiere in Rome of *The Serpent,* as the performance piece was now entitled. At this point all the open questions were closed, the final choices made. Ascendant was van Itallie's vision of the necessities of a finished and public work. Chaikin, who had mediated between the writer and the actors as long as performance was not upon him, had to support van Itallie's choices for the verbal and kinetic architecture of the piece. What had once belonged to the troupe in common looked at the time of the opening very like van Itallie's property; to many of the actors it seemed that Chaikin had given the piece away.

By June, after a month of touring, the demoralization was staggering. The actors moved around Europe like tourists, hanging out in groups of four and five, seeing the sights, and coming together only when necessary—for travel, rehearsal, and performance. In Zurich, Miss Worley made an attempt to get the troupe to air grievances and hopefully to heal some of the rifts. But without Chaikin's imparting a sense of urgency (he had told the troupe in December that "I don't consider personal conflicts within the group to be part of my responsibility") the meeting could accomplish little.

To me it is an unprovable certainty that the bad relations within the company vitiated the European performances of *The Serpent*. The production was impressive—a serious and often startling innovation. But it lacked clarity and emotional power as an ensemble work. *The Serpent* did not live in performance until the following January, when the troupe took it up again in New York.

During the summer, van Itallie polished the play for publication, and when the actors approached it again they worked from a scenario and text which was established but not inviolable. Chaikin and the actors amended the production, dropping passages to which they no longer felt a personal connection, developing some new ones. They were alone again; van Itallie trusted them; the ensemble was gradually re-established. The atmosphere of work was entirely different. The troupe had had a respite since finishing the tour in August; the core of the company had gone to Arizona to film a scene in Antonioni's *Zabriskie Point*. When work resumed in November, it occurred in a large new loft being paid for out of a grant of $54,000 from the Ford Foundation and another of $7,500 from the National Endowment on the Arts. The loft was located at 14th Street and 6th Avenue, catty-corner from the former home of the Living Theatre whose auditorium Chaikin had borrowed for the first meeting of the Open Theatre in 1963. When, in January and February 1969, the company gave free performances of *The Serpent* at the loft, the piece emerged as the densest and richest of the Open Theatre's works.

The Serpent does not so much tell the story of Adam as project kinetic images related to the story's monumental events. The serpent tempts Eve, Eve succumbs; Eve tempts Adam, Adam succumbs; God casts them out: Eden is erased on every level—physical, psychic, spiritual; Paradise is lost. You do not have to believe that the events occurred; the Open Theatre does not believe that the events occurred. A myth is a story which you affirm with the heart even as you reject it with the head; its realm is the subconscious, and its power is emotional. The brain may attack the events and the concepts of a myth, but the associated images and rhythms sieve quickly through the brain to reach the heart. (This is the more true of myth which is enacted, for it addresses not the imagination but the senses.) The events of biblical myth already exist in our hearts; we have heard the story before. Indeed, we grew up with the story, and within it:

> Old stories
> Have a secret.
> They are a prison.
> Someone is locked inside them.
> Sometimes, when it's very quiet,
> I can hear him breathing.
>
> (from the text)

In performance, the Open Theatre's story of Adam is very quiet; as you listen carefully, you hear yourself inside it. With that recognition, you begin to mourn: for Adam and Eve and their loss of Eden, for yourself and your own loss.

The Serpent presents the creation and fall of man in six episodes, beginning with the creation of Eve and finishing with the begetting of the generations of Adam. Each episode is a unit compounded of visual and aural images created by the actors with their bodies alone. (There are some primitive percussion instruments and a bag of apples.) The scenes are interrelated through the repetition of sensory motifs: we see Eve's reach for the apple in Adam's gesture accusing her before the angry God; we see both of those events in the supplicating gesture of Abel's ghost; we see all of them in the man's reach for his woman in the Begatting Scene. I have counted a dozen repetitions of that one motif; there are many other motifs, aural as well as visual. The play's kinetic vocabulary, which the verbal text serves as a score, rather than the usual reverse, endows the biblical events with the character of mental pictures in motion like dim imaginings, which will not go away, in some deep recess of the mind. "Whatever I know/I know it without words," someone tells us.

Van Itallie's device of the chorus—three or four women who stand apart from the biblical events—reinforces the reflective mode of presentation. The women are contemporary figures who see the story of Adam in their mind's eye, who listen for their breathing in the old story. They meditate on their difficulties—peculiarly modern, recognizable plaints: alienation from others and disintegration of self. These women are the accursed descendants of Eve, and they know that they cannot move in a direction where the curse will not abide. Like the lemmings to whose death migration they allude in a central passage, they are locked into the race forward. And while they cannot regain Paradise, they cannot forget about it either. To suffer is not only to feel pain, but to know that one is denied access to painlessness.

> Accursed, you shall glimpse Eden
> All the days of your life.
> But you shall not come again.
> And if you should come,
> You would not know it.
>
> (from the text)

The chorus of women is not the only contemporary aspect of *The Serpent*. A crucial scene, the basis for which had been laid by van Itallie and Levy in the assassination workshop, presents the assassinations of John Kennedy, Martin Luther King, and Robert Kennedy in ritualized form. From this scene, which occurs early in the play, depends the rest of the action: the biblical portions of *The Serpent* are, as it were, an investigation of the psychic climate out of which the Kennedy-King-Kennedy violence sprang. The alienation, disintegration, and impotence inherent in the violent acts of modern America are *described* by the contemporary episode, and *defined* by the biblical scenes. In *The Serpent,* the story of Adam prefigures the very real acts of our contemporary public life. It is in the relationships of the play's parts that I see its unique character and a recognizable synthesis of the inner and the outer strains of the Open Theatre's work.

The Open Theatre calls *The Serpent* a ceremony. As the actors project their personal version of the story of Adam they are the priests of the offering. As the women of the chorus mediate the events for us they are the priests of the lesson. The members of the troupe have examined the myth of Eden for its personal relevance to themselves and have ceremonialized what they discovered. Their presentation has great emotional power for us who look on. As a work *The Serpent* defeats the brain, that repressive organ by which we keep ourselves detached from an inner truth; it re-creates the mythic events which led to the isolation and supremacy of the brain over the body and the spirit. A ceremony is a way of expressing things held to be true by all those present, but not accessible through discourse or rational disclosure. *The Serpent* is a ceremony of mourning—a lay requiem or kaddish, in which our Adamite heritage, which is loss of Eden, is rediscovered by the actors and by ourselves. Like many ceremonies, it is a form of revelation.

At the loft performances *The Serpent* seemed to touch the spectators in some secret place where they had not known sensation before. They seemed to be experiencing wonder and sometimes awe—legitimate achievements in the theatre, yet so rare as to sound alien in the context of play-going. This was not due merely to the awesome themes with which the play dealt, but primarily to the uncommon control, fed by an unusual degree of personal conviction, which the troupe brought to its performing. No longer a raw company, the actors had gained an ability to share in performance their private targets. Thanks to the period of re-working the play, they had also regained their commitment to a play of which the core was their creation. The troupe's task in successive performances would be to keep feeding that commitment to those skills.

EPILOGUE

This book stops here as I break into my habit of looking at the Open Theatre and listening to Chaikin in order to do some other things. With *The Serpent,* the Open Theatre achieved a certain celebrity, and Chaikin became a personage in the theatre. The troupe goes forward with other research and new projects which will enter new territory. The moment that Chaikin repeats something it bores him, and since his workshop is the environment which he has created out of his own needs, he and the actors are always moving on. There will be new members, old members newly energized, and contacts with new outside influences. The Open Theatre will evolve. Surely it is already unrecognizable.